ELEMENTARY
SEWING
SKILLS

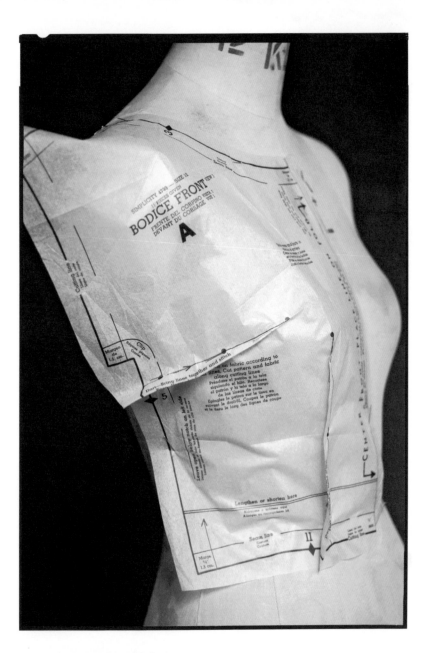

ELEMENTARY
SEWING
SKILLS

CAROLYN N.K.DENHAM

words and pictures by
RODERICK FIELD

MERCHANT & MILLS

PAVILION

CONTENTS

INTRODUCTION

Elementary skills are at the beginning of our endeavours. They are not comprehensive or complete, but are the foundations of learning and the first steps towards building a dependable, useful knowledge base that informs our efforts and allows us to progress. We have been ruthless in paring down the vast library of sewing information that exists and presenting you with fundamental, basic and indispensable nuggets of wisdom for you to digest and master.

Merchant & Mills believe in sewing – seriously. Yet we also believe that sewing should be fun and rewarding, not filled with fear and dread of failure, like dieting or parallel parking under pressure. This book aims to draw out ability, encourage creativity and bring you, the reader, something marvellous to show for your efforts beyond pin-pricked fingers and a carpet covered in lint.

We will guide you through the key elements of using the sewing machine, understanding garment construction, in theory and in practice, and using sewing patterns to make the clothes you want to wear. This books hopes to be your ever-ready tutor, to elaborate on troublesome methods or to offer a simple solution to a challenging task. With due application, it will enable you to grow in ability and confidence while all the time preparing you to face a more complex and thorough book on sewing.

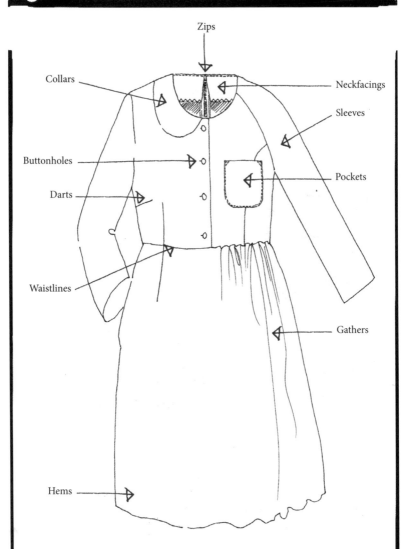

Zips

Collars

Neckfacings

Sleeves

Buttonholes

Pockets

Darts

Waistlines

Gathers

Hems

In this book, we will be covering some of the basic techniques in dressmaking, preparation, construction and finishing.

ORDER OF MAKING

The structure of this book roughly follows the order in which you would make a garment. First of all we consider the essential dressmaking tools and materials: the sewing machine, other useful tools and the fabric. We then move on to explaining pattern pieces and garment construction.

→ All markings are transferred from the pattern pieces to the fabric.

→ All fusible interfacing is cut and carefully ironed on the wrong side of the fabric.

→ You should work on the flat where possible.

The most important lesson is that any steps that can be completed before the fabric is constructed into a three-dimensional garment should be done first as it is much easier to work on a flat body piece. Darts and patch pockets should be tackled first so that you are working on the flat. Back seams can be joined; if the back has no waist seams and there is a zip to be inserted this can be done now. Shoulder seams come next. Depending on the design, any neck facings or collars can be made at this point so again you are working on the flat.

Then we move on to side seams and in-seam pockets. Armholes can be finished or sleeves inserted. Waist seams are joined, zips or facings that cross the waist seams are completed, and necklines and collars may need to be done now.

Buttonholes and buttons are tackled last before hemming the finished garment.

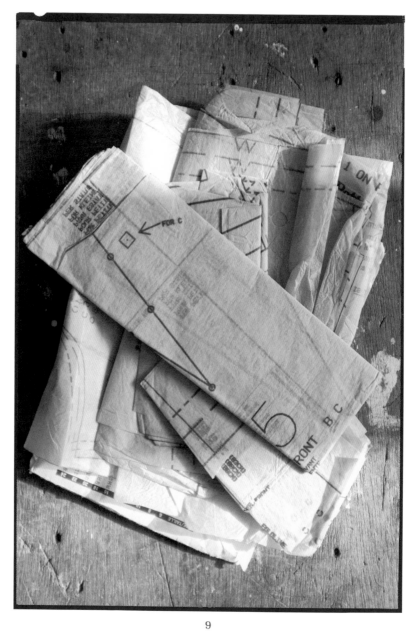

THE SEWING MACHINE

A beginner needs a sewing machine with a good straight stitch, zigzag and buttonhole. Your machine does not need computer programs, embroidery features, smartphone apps or anything else.

A removable sewing machine arm is useful as it allows you to sew armholes and cuffs more easily. A sewing machine set into a table allows you much more control and is generally considered better.

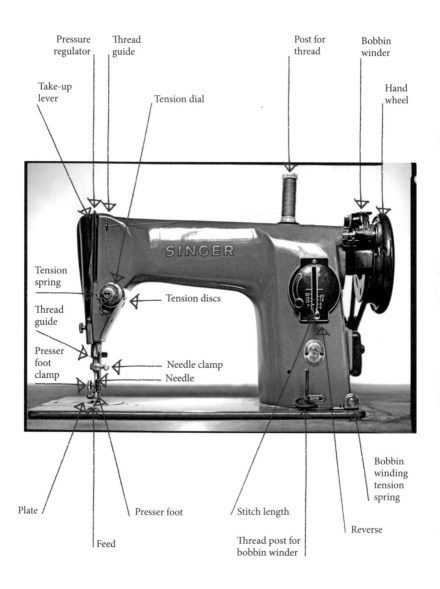

Pressure regulator

Thread guide

Post for thread

Bobbin winder

Take-up lever

Tension dial

Hand wheel

Tension spring

Tension discs

Thread guide

Presser foot clamp

Needle clamp

Needle

Plate

Presser foot

Stitch length

Bobbin winding tension spring

Reverse

Feed

Thread post for bobbin winder

THREADING AND THREAD TYPES

Cotton or sew-all (polyester) will serve most purposes. Avoid cheap threads, as they may unravel and shed fluff around the needle eye as you sew, before snapping. Thread is not a place where you should try to make savings!

THREADING THE MACHINE

Although sewing machines can look very complicated at first sight, they all follow the same basic principles and you will find that all models share certain common features.

To thread the machine, lift up the presser foot. The thread will only pull through the tension discs if the presser foot is raised.

The basic principle for threading is across, down, around and hooked, up, down and through the needle. This is always the same, no matter what model of sewing machine you have.

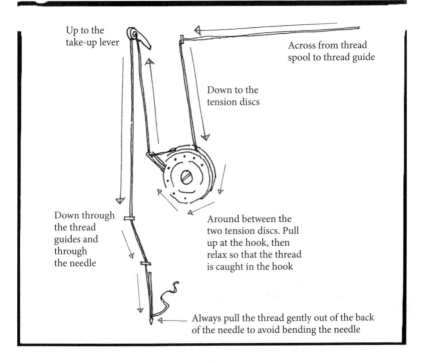

Up to the take-up lever

Across from thread spool to thread guide

Down to the tension discs

Down through the thread guides and through the needle

Around between the two tension discs. Pull up at the hook, then relax so that the thread is caught in the hook

Always pull the thread gently out of the back of the needle to avoid bending the needle

SEWING MACHINE NEEDLES

There are three basic types of sewing machine needles:

→ a: sharp all-standard fabrics
→ b: ball-point knits
→ c: chiselled leather and vinyls.

Needles are available in sizes from 70 to 110. Choose the size based on the weight of the fabric and change the needle regularly:

→ lightweight fabrics: 70–80
→ medium-weight fabrics: 80–90
→ heavy-weight fabrics: 90–100
→ heavy denims, canvas: 110.

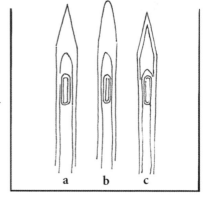

The top of the needle has one flat side that slots into the post. The flat side normally goes to the back; however, with some older machines it will go to one side. The machine will not sew if the needle is inserted incorrectly.

INSERTING A NEEDLE INTO THE NEEDLE CLAMP

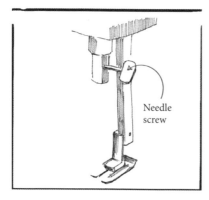

Needle screw

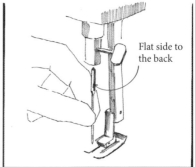

Flat side to the back

1 To insert the needle, you will first need to loosen the needle clamp.

2 With the flat side of the needle towards the back, push the needle as far as it will go into the clamp.

FEED AND FOOT PRESSURE

The feed is under the plate directly under the presser foot. The feed moves the fabric along with each stitch. How much it moves is controlled by the stitch length.

The foot pressure is controlled on the top or with a dial on the side. The tighter the screw or higher the number, the greater the pressure applied.

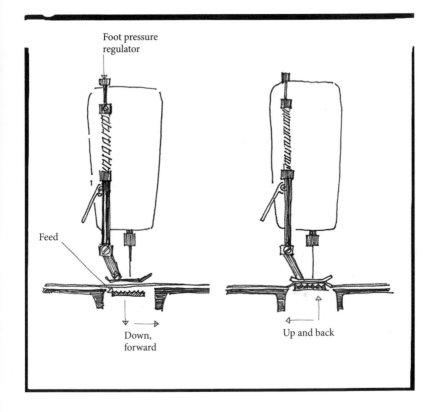

Foot pressure regulator

Feed

Down, forward

Up and back

THE CORRECT FOOT PRESSURE

Applying not enough foot pressure will result in wobbly stitching or sometimes skipped stitches as the fabric is not controlled enough. Conversely, applying too much foot pressure can be one of the causes of uneven seams.

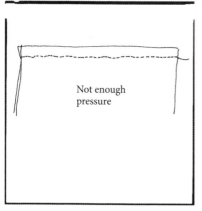

Not enough pressure

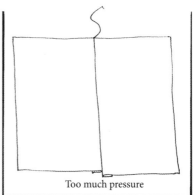

Too much pressure

UNEVEN SEAMS

The feed dogs pull the bottom layer of fabric more than the top layer, so it is not uncommon to end the seam unevenly. To overcome this effect, hold the fabric in your right hand with thumb under and fingers over, and then rotate your hand slightly upwards. This helps to retard the movement of the lower layer just a little, and helps to keep the edges aligned.

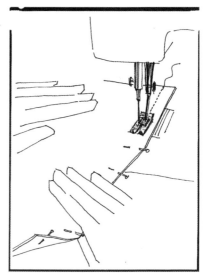

BOBBINS

There are two basic types of bobbin case: the older style built-in case, or the more common removable case. The built-in style requires only the bobbin to be lifted out or dropped in, whereas the removable case must be lifted out before the bobbin can be removed.

Some machines do not require the bobbin to be removed; the bobbin winding is done inside the machine.

Be aware that there are several size variations in bobbins and they will only fit the right machine.

The needle must be disengaged before winding on the bobbin; this is done by turning the smaller wheel at the side of the machine towards you while holding the larger wheel still.

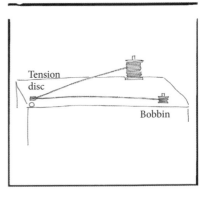

The bobbin winding gubbins can be set up differently on each machine, but the principle is always the same: from the thread spool through a tension disc to the bobbin.

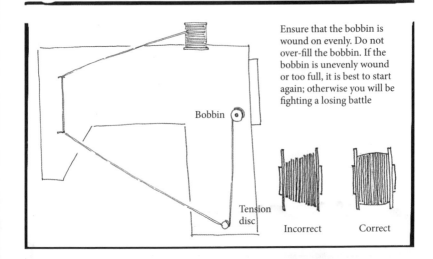

Ensure that the bobbin is wound on evenly. Do not over-fill the bobbin. If the bobbin is unevenly wound or too full, it is best to start again; otherwise you will be fighting a losing battle

Bobbin

Tension disc

Incorrect   Correct

GETTING THE RIGHT TENSION

The stitch should be even on both sides. If the top tension is too loose, the stitch will form on the bottom. If the top tension is too tight, the stitch will form on the top.

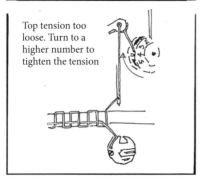

Top tension too loose. Turn to a higher number to tighten the tension

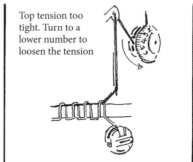

Top tension too tight. Turn to a lower number to loosen the tension

ALTERING THE BOTTOM TENSION

The bottom tension is more difficult to alter. Only very slight adjustments are needed and, as there is no guide, you can end up going around in circles. Therefore, do not alter the bottom tension unless you absolutely have to.

Both built-in and removable bobbin cases have a small adjustment screw on the side. The general rule is to turn the screw clockwise to increase tension and anti-clockwise to decrease. It might be helpful to remember: 'righty tighty, lefty loosey'.

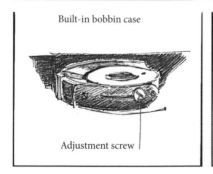

Built-in bobbin case

Adjustment screw

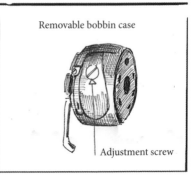

Removable bobbin case

Adjustment screw

MACHINE FEET

There are hundreds of different feet available that have all sorts of functions, from blind hemming to binding. However, there are just three basic types that you really need: zipper foot (left), straight stitch foot (middle) and zigzag (right).

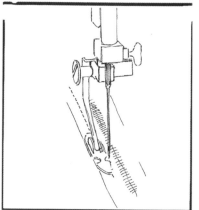

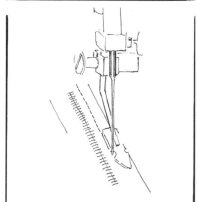

The zigzag foot can be used to make both zigzag stitch and straight stitch, which consequently reduces your need to just two types of feet.

The zigzag foot can therefore be the foot of choice for almost every task, and will only need to be changed when inserting a zip.

The zipper foot is very narrow; it is able to slide from side to side, allowing the bulk of the zip to stay out of the way of the foot.

The zipper foot can be positioned either side of the needle. It can also be used for stitching in piping or where there is bulk on one side of the seam.

STRAIGHT STITCH AND ZIGZAG

These are the two stitches we are most interested in: the straight stitch is used for seams while the zigzag is for neatening seams and creating buttonholes.

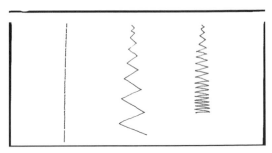

STRAIGHT STITCH LENGTH

This is controlled by a dial on the front of the machine. The higher the number, the longer the stitch. As a general rule, use a short stitch for fine fabrics and a slightly longer stitch for heavier fabrics. Only use the longest stitch for gathering.

The zigzag stitch can be controlled in both length (using the same dial as the straight stitch length) and in width. The higher the number, the wider the stitch. The general rule is to use a narrower stitch for fine fabrics and a wider stitch for heavier fabrics or fabrics that fray.

CLEANING AND MAINTENANCE

The bobbin case and the feed teeth can quickly become clogged up with fluff, so it is important to clean them regularly. Brush them out thoroughly with the tip of a firm brush.

To maintain your sewing machine in good working order, take care to oil it regularly. Before using it again, run through several pieces of scraps to get rid of any excess oil.

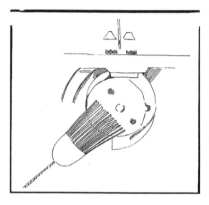

TROUBLESHOOTING

If there is a problem with the machine, it can most likely by doing one of these three things:

→ Rethread the machine. It may have become unthreaded or slipped out of the tension dials.

→ Rethread the bobbin. Also check whether there are any threads caught in the bobbin housing and that the bobbin is wound on evenly.

→ Change the needle. A blunt needle can create havoc, making skipped stitches and causing the thread to break. Also make sure the needle is the right size for the fabric (see page 13).

If there is still a problem, refer to the sewing machine manual.

TOOLS

You will need some good-quality basic tools in addition to your sewing machine. It may be tempting to go mad spending on lots of wonderful sewing tools, but it is prudent to invest well in the items you will actually need to get started. All dressmakers will find particular tools that they prefer to use and find the most comfortable. As your skills grow, you will want to add to your tools depending on the kind of work you do.

SCISSORS

Scissors are the dressmaker's constant companion. Ideally, you will have the right pair for the task at hand, from cutting out cloth to snipping threads or opening up buttonholes.

We suggest starting with some quality shears that can be sharpened or reset as required and will potentially last a lifetime. Add to this a nice sharp pair of small scissors and you will be good to go on most projects. When you find you need something more specialist, that is the time to add to your toolkit.

A pair of 8-inch scissors is easy to handle and will tackle tasks such as cutting out cloth and trimming seams.

Sharp, small scissors will allow you to get right to the bottom of the thread to trim, as the blades are thin. They can

also be used for opening buttonholes. Household scissors can be used for cutting out card patterns. Never use your shears on anything other than cloth and keep them safely away from people who don't sew!

PINS

Nickel-plated steel pins are the best. Choose a slim pin and replace them regularly, as blunt or thick pins can pull the threads of the fabric. Pins come in a range of sizes:

➤ For standard fabrics: dressmaker's pins 0.60mm–0.65mm

➤ For fine fabrics: 0.44mm or less (often called silk pins)

➤ For thick fabrics choose an extra-long strong pin, with a diameter of 0.70mm (often called quilter's pins)

➤ The very best pin cushion is filled with an emery powder to keep pins sharp.

CHALK

NEEDLES

Tailor's chalk is used for transferring marks from the pattern pieces to the cloth (see page 46). It is a good idea to mark the wrong side of each cut pattern piece with an X. This saves time and confusion, avoiding the easy mistake of putting the wrong sides together. Keep the chalk sharp using a craft knife.

Most common household needles are called sharps and often come in a mixed pack. These will cover most of your needs. Long, slim needles are used for tacking, whereas a short, fine needle gives a neat and even stitch for hand-finishing. Choose the thickness of your needle depending on the weight of your fabric.

OTHER TOOLS

A bamboo point turner is useful for turning out corners and collars. Avoid using scissors or a pencil for this job, although a knitting needle or chopstick could make a reasonable substitute.

A good-quality tape measure will not stretch and become inaccurate. Find one with a metal end, marked with both inches and centimetres.

Other useful items are safety pins, for threading elastic or drawstrings; a steam iron (keep it clean and full of water); and a pressing cloth of fine linen cotton.

FABRIC

Once you have narrowed down your choices to the one fabulous fabric you are going to use, there are some basic rules of engagement to consider. Foremost of these is preparation. Some fabrics, particularly cottons, need to be washed beforehand as they may shrink.

CHOOSING FABRIC

Selecting the right fabric is a skill learned by way of many mistakes. The better quality the fabric, the better the result. It is easy to be tempted by wonderful prints and great colours, but check in with your inner wardrobe. What colours or prints do you actually wear? Which brands do you like and what kind of fabrics do they choose?

COTTON

The easiest fabrics to use are cottons. They press well and generally have a tight weave, allowing easy trimming of seams. They tend to be stable and do not stretch, so are easy to stitch. Quality cottons are a delight to work with and, if finished well, can look great, while cheap printed cottons are great for fun summer dresses that don't ask too much. Note that some cottons can look like typical dressmaking fabrics without body, drape or interest and so can be a safe yet uninspiring choice.

LINEN

This is a great dressmaker's fabric that oozes sophistication. The better the quality, the more refined the result. Linens can have a more open weave, requiring extra attention when finishing or trimming seams. Press well with a damp cloth.

WOOL

This requires more practice, as it can stretch and be difficult to press well. Steer clear of very flat wools that look beautiful on the bolt but are very unforgiving and will show every fault. Instead choose something with a woolly or textured finish; these will hide a multitude of sins.

WASHING FABRIC

It is advisable to wash fabric before you work with it, for three reasons:

1 Washing removes size (a starch finish used in the weaving process that makes the fabric feel stiff).

2 Shrinkage. Many fabrics will shrink a little in the first wash, which will spell disaster if you have already made up your garment.

3 Colour loss. Some colours may fade with the first wash, which can affect the choice of matching thread.

As a general rule, wash cottons before use. The more expensive the fabric, the less need for a pre-wash, as the shrinking process and size will have been eliminated by the mill.

Linens do not hold colour well. If you choose to wash linen rather than dry-clean it, you will affect the finish of the fabric.

Many wools are dry-clean only, but most mixed blends can be washed.

If you have washed your fabric, press it while still damp to take out any creases.

FABRIC WIDTHS

Fabric comes in varying widths; these are the most common:

→ 90cm: A very narrow width, often seen in hand-loomed fabrics or precious fabrics such as silk brocade.

→ 120cm: Silk generally comes in this width. You will also find many hand-printed or hand-blocked fabrics at this width.

→ 140cm and 150cm: These are the most common widths for dress and soft furnishing fabrics.

FABRICS WITH A NAP

Fabrics with a nap have a pile or direction of weave (think of suede). This means that your pattern pieces will need to be cut out all in the same direction. You will need more of any given fabric as you have fewer layout options. Obvious examples of this type of fabric are velvets and cords, but many fabrics have a very subtle nap so examine thoroughly before cutting. Fold the fabric in half with wrong sides together and then in half again. The two sides should look the same; if they don't, the fabric has a nap.

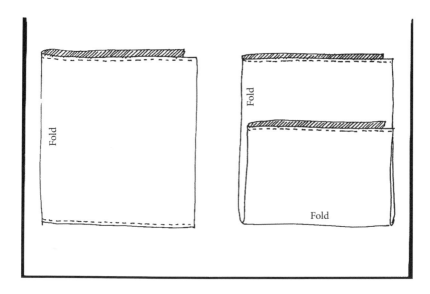

PREPARING FABRIC

All fabrics should be well pressed and folded ready for cutting out. Straighten up at least one end before folding. There are several methods to get the end absolutely straight. For a perfect straight line at right angles to the selvedge edge, cottons can be torn right across. With more loosely woven fabrics, you can determine a straight line by snipping into the selvedge edge and pulling on one weft thread, creating a visible pucker from edge to edge. Fabric with checks or simple patterns can be cut straight simply by following the pattern like graph paper.

Most patterns are cut so that the warp runs down the pattern from head to toe. Patterns that are cut parallel to the weft or diagonally across the fabric (on the bias) will hang and drape in a very different way.

WORKING WITH FABRIC

It is a good idea to sew a practice seam on a scrap of fabric to see whether the needle size you have is correct, whether there is any stretch on the cloth, and that the tension on the machine is set correctly.

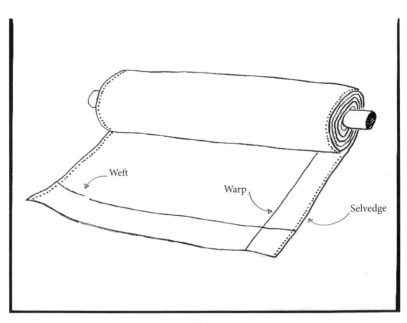

THE PATTERN

For the uninitiated, a pattern is like a jigsaw of the garment you are going to make, printed on one or several large sheets of tissue paper ready for you to cut out in your size. For many decades, dressmaking patterns have been presented in this way, featuring graduating lines, from size tiny to rather bigger, folded into an envelope with a set of instructions telling you how to translate this tissue wonder into a functional and desirable garment.

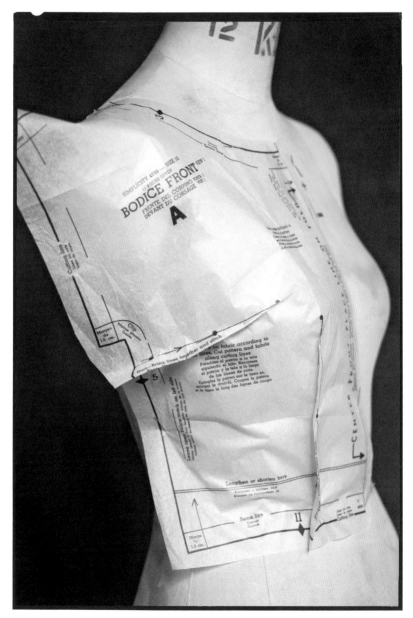

HANDLING THE PATTERN

Pattern marking can look a bit daunting but each pattern will have a key to understanding what the marks mean. These are some of the most common markings:

BEFORE CUTTING MARKINGS

a: Pattern piece name and number. Use these to identify the pieces you need.

b: The double parallel lines indicate where the pattern can be lengthened or shortened.

LAYOUT LINES

c: The grain line indicates where the pattern piece will be laid in relation to the selvedge edge.

d: Where a pattern piece has no seam, to create one whole piece it is placed on a fold.

e: Cutting lines can be marked with a pair of scissors.

f: Most sewing patterns are multi-grade (multi-size) and have all sizes printed as a nest on one sheet of paper. Beware of the myriad markings on these and ensure you use the correct markings and lines for the size you are working to. Before cutting out the pattern, examine it thoroughly to understand where the cutting lines and markings are for your size.

CONSTRUCTION MARKINGS

g: Marks along the cutting lines: notches along the cutting line are match points for lining up seams during construction.

h: Marks inside the cutting line: dots are to be marked with tailor's tacks or chalk to indicate darts, buttonholes, pocket positions, tucks and seam details such as zip positions.

On the reverse of your pattern envelope, expect to see a size chart and a guide to how much fabric each size takes. There will be a line drawing showing the silhouette and detailing of each garment. Study this carefully to understand how the garment will look – it often gives more information than the drawing or photograph on the front. Note the information on the need for any interfacing, zips or buttons and how many and what size these may be.

Handle the pattern with care, as it will rip easily. Before committing to cutting out, study the instructions as you would a map in order to see where you are going and whether you need anything else. Take care to stick to the correct line for your size!

Pattern instructions can vary greatly on clarity and information. Many will presume some prior knowledge and will not instruct on every detail.

PATTERN MARKINGS

Before Cutting Markings

a

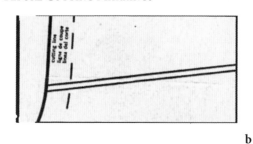

b

Layout Lines

c

d

e

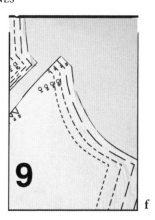

f

Construction Markings

g

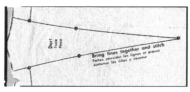

h

WHAT'S IN THE PATTERN ENVELOPE?

Along with the pattern and instructions, the pattern includes a diagram of the pattern pieces. Each pattern piece is numbered. Use this guide to keep track of how many pattern pieces you have, especially any small ones.

PATTERN PIECES FOR A DRESS

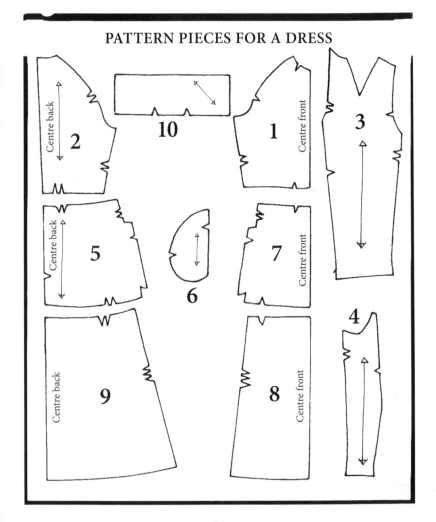

Following this there are layout cutting plans. Each one will be for a different width of fabric and often there will be variations depending on size.

Most importantly, there is the paper pattern. Before you start, cut out each pattern piece and press out any creases with a warm dry iron.

UNDERSTANDING CUTTING PLANS

Some of the pattern pieces will be cut on the fold so that when they are opened up they make one piece. Often the fabric can be folded and then refolded in a different way to provide the most economical use of the cutting plan.

Both selvedges folded to the centre

Selvedges folded together

One selvedge folded to the centre

A typical cutting plan shows where the fabric is folded and the best placement of the pattern pieces for each width of fabric.

Understanding this diagram will help you to achieve the most economical use of fabric. The fabric may be refolded more than once.

This picture shows one layout with one straightforward fold. The other layout shows one side folded to the centre.

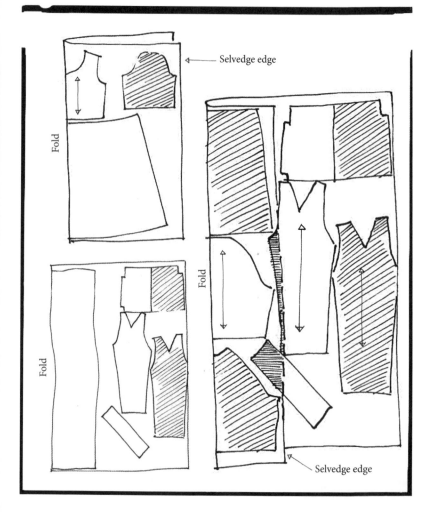

→ Diagonal stripes indicate that the pattern piece is placed with the printed side down.

→ Plain pieces are placed with the printed side up.

→ One plain and one striped piece together mean that the fabric will be refolded so that the pattern can be cut on the fold.

→ Pattern pieces half on and half off the fabric mean that, after cutting out all the other pieces, you need to unfold the fabric to cut out this piece.

→ An asterisk indicates that there are special instructions for the pattern pieces.

→ An interrupted line indicates that the pattern piece will be cut out more than once.

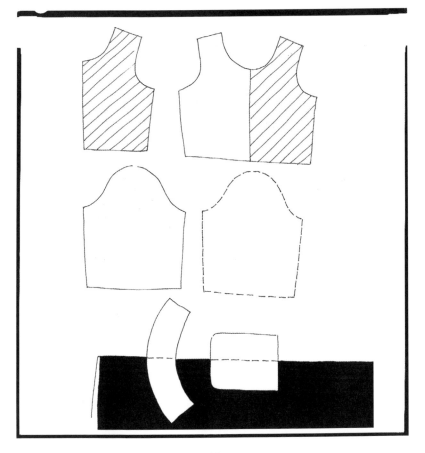

PATTERN POSITION AND GRAIN LINES

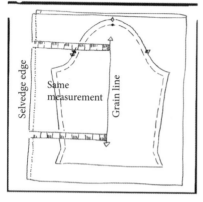

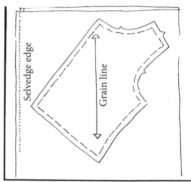

All pattern pieces are marked with a grain line. This is placed parallel to the selvedge. Measure the distance from each end of the grain line arrow to the selvedge edge, adjusting the pattern piece until both ends of the arrow are the same distance away.

Grain lines may not always be straight on the pattern piece; bias-cut pieces will have the grain marked diagonally across the pattern.

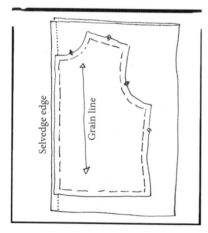

The selvedge edge can vary significantly depending on the fabric being used. Some are very deep and are not considered part of the fabric width. If they are flat and neat they can be incorporated into the seam allowance, but be careful not to go inside the seam allowance where they might show.

PINNING OUT

Start pinning out at the fold of the fabric, starting at the corners and then along the fold. Make sure the pattern is right on the fold and not just under or just over, as this will alter the size of the final garment. Smooth out the pattern and pin each remaining corner before pinning out the rest of the pattern. Pin enough so that the pattern will not lift up when cutting out.

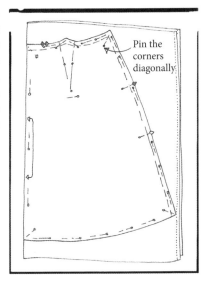

Pin the corners diagonally

CUTTING OUT

The cutting line is the thickest dark line on the outside of the pattern. Keep one hand close to the scissors when cutting out to prevent the pattern or cloth lifting up. Use long firm strokes with the scissors. Good sharp scissors will make cutting out much easier. Take your time and cut out accurately and neatly.

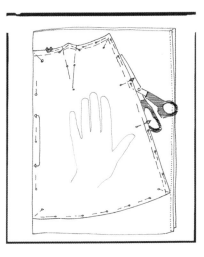

MARKING NOTCHES

Marking key points with notches is essential in matching up seams in construction. Some notches are double notches; this generally indicates the back. Cut into the notch or around the notch, as preferred.

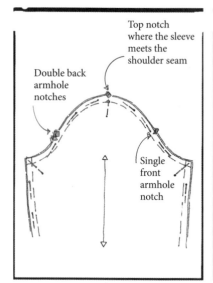

Double back armhole notches

Top notch where the sleeve meets the shoulder seam

Single front armhole notch

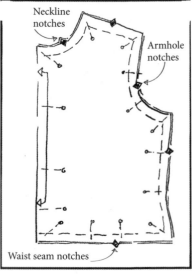

Neckline notches

Armhole notches

Waist seam notches

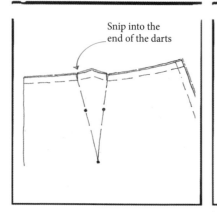

Snip into the end of the darts

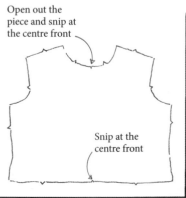

Open out the piece and snip at the centre front

Snip at the centre front

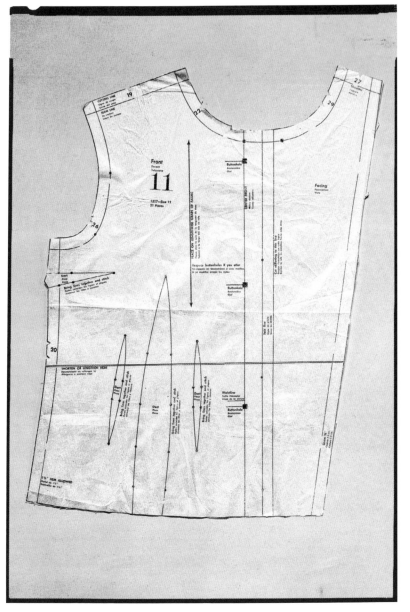

TRANSFERRING PATTERN MARKINGS TO THE FABRIC

TAILOR'S TACKS

These take more time, but are useful for fabrics that don't mark well with chalk.

Transfer the markings before removing the pattern pieces.

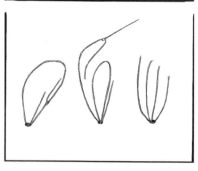

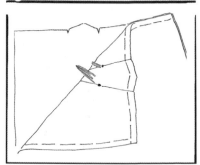

1 Using a double thread, stitch a loop through the pattern and all the layers of fabric. Snip the top of the loop. Repeat for all dots.

2 Carefully lift off the pattern without pulling out any threads.

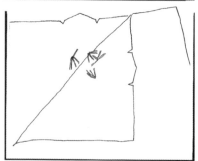

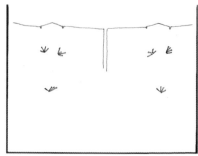

3 Lift off the top layer of fabric, snipping each thread in between the two layers so that threads are on both sides.

MARKING WITH TAILOR'S CHALK

Tailor's chalk is available in different colours. If marking on the right side, always test the chalk on the fabric as it can permanently mark some fabric.

Darts are marked on the wrong side of the fabric.

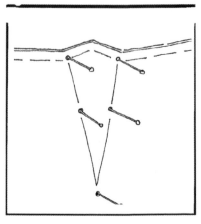

1 Push pins through the pattern and all layers of fabric.

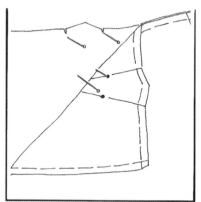

2 Gently lift off the pattern, forcing the pin heads through the pattern piece.

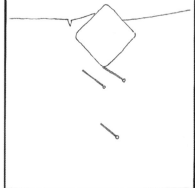

3 Mark each pin position with a chalk dot on the wrong side of all fabric pieces. These dots can now be joined up with chalk and a ruler to give a clear stitching line.

PRESSING

Pressing is as important as sewing; expect to spend more time at the ironing board than at the sewing machine. A good powerful steam iron will help. Press every stage of the stitching, as a badly pressed garment will always look homemade.

There are many tools to help with pressing, but start with the basics to make sure that every seam and detail is pressed perfectly before moving on to the next stage.

TIPS ON PRESSING

To find the best temperature and method, do some tests before pressing the garment. Always use a pressing cloth for wools and linens as they will develop a shine if pressed on the right side. After pressing and when the fabric is cooled, lift the garment off the ironing board and let it hang in your hand to see if it is pressed perfectly. Over pressing will make the garment look laboured and shabby.

Pressing is different from ironing and requires a different action. Do not slide the iron along; put the iron down, then lift up, move along and put it down again.

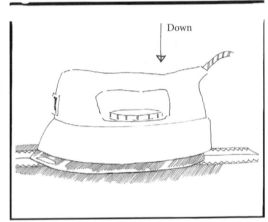

Down

After pressing, let the fabric cool completely before lifting it off the ironing board. This will set the heat and steam.

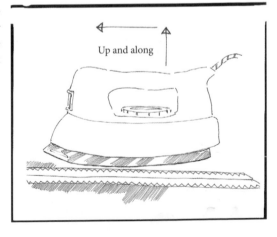

Up and along

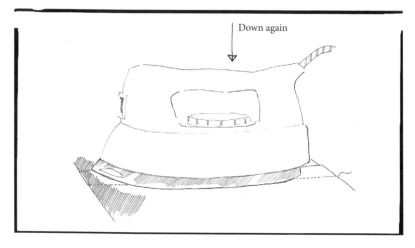

Press the stitching flat before pressing a seam open to achieve the best results. This is called melding the stitches or setting them down.

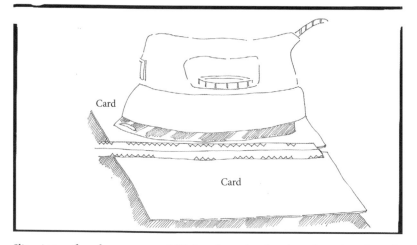

Slip pieces of card or a scrap of fabric under darts and other details to prevent them showing through to the other side of the garment.

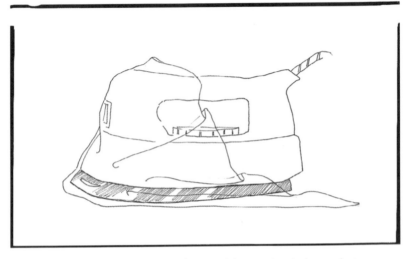

With the cloth under the iron, drape the rest of the pressing cloth over the iron.

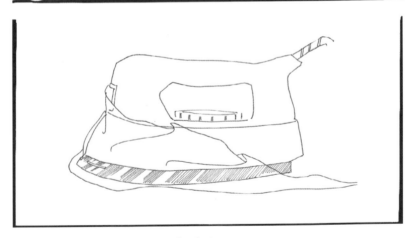

The cloth will continue to move under the iron as you press.

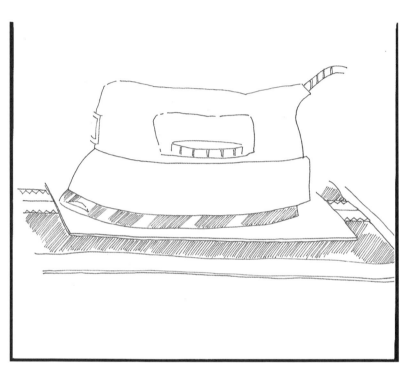

A pressing cloth is simply a large damp scrap of linen or cotton – linen is the best as it retains more water. It is always used when pressing the right side of the fabric to protect the fabric (many fabrics will take on a shine if not protected).

Keep the cloth damp but not wet, as this might shrink some fabrics.

When pressing wool or patch pocket details, place a scrap of the wool under the garment and another scrap under the iron as a pressing cloth; this will help to keep the fabric from flattening too much.

HAND STITCHING

Although there is an infinite number of hand stitches, from the most elaborate to the very simplest, and each with a perfect use, there are just a few that are truly indispensable. In this chapter, we cover only the essential techniques of tacking (basting), cross stitch, slip stitch and running stitch. You can get by just with these stitches for most sewing demands.

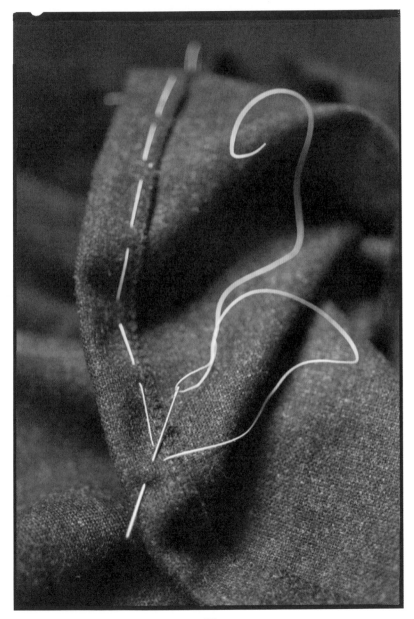

TACKING

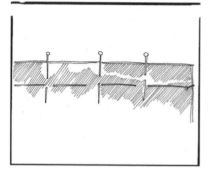

Tacking (also called basting) is a long, even stitch that is used to temporarily hold layers of fabric together. Use a long needle to make several stitches at once.

Tacking is used for two different reasons. The first is to tack a garment together for fitting. It is more accurate and less painful than pinning. The second is to hold difficult seams together before stitching. Tacking is pulled out when the stitching or fitting is complete.

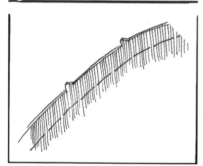

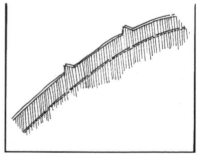

Tacking for fitting should be done on the stitching line.

Tacking to hold difficult seams should be done just inside the seam allowance. Do not stitch on top of the tacking line, as it can be difficult to remove. Use a contrast thread so it is easy to see when pulling out.

SLIP STITCH

Slip stitch is used to bring two folded edges together. It is almost invisible and can be used to close bag linings or to close a cushion. Use a short needle such as a quilter or between. Stitch from right to left, passing the needle through the fold of the seam close to the edge. Make one small stitch directly opposite on the other folded edge, bring the needle through the fold right next to the edge and repeat.

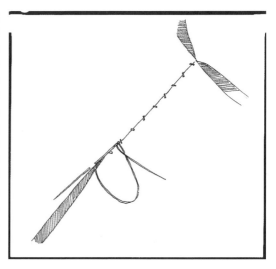

CROSS STITCH

A cross stitch is a simple, secure stitch used on facing edges where one spot needs to be sewn to hold the edges in place on the inside of a garment. It is usually stitched several times.

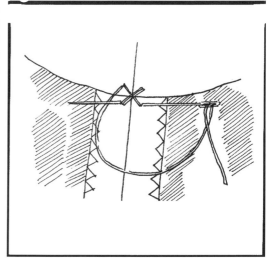

SEAMS

Good straight seams lie at the heart of all garment construction. Simple as they may be, attention and patience are paramount in achieving a well-finished, professional result. Wobbly seams charm no one. If your first seam is off, everything that you build upon it will be compromised. Understanding your fabric, correct thread tension, appropriate stitch size and steady machine control are the prerequisites for seams to be proud of. Respect the cloth – it is important not to stretch the seam as this will show. It is also crucial to press all the seams really well. Expect to spend as much time pressing as sewing.

HOW TO MAKE PLAIN SEAMS

1 Before starting to construct the garment, make sure that you have the correct needle for the type of fabric. Needles that are too thick will cause pulling on the threads of the fabric. Needles that are too thin will break.

2 Choose the right thread colour. Unreel a short length of thread and lay it on top of your fabric to see whether it is a good match.

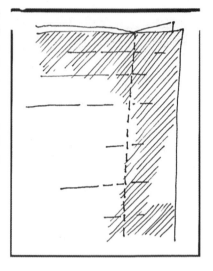

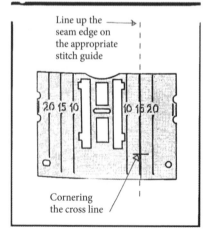

Line up the ⟶ seam edge on the appropriate stitch guide

2.0 15 10   10 15 2.0

Cornering the cross line

TIPS

⇢ Don't watch the needle when stitching; instead, look at the seam edge and the foot-plate guide.

⇢ Don't start stitching right at the beginning of the seam. The seam may be pulled down into the needle hole, especially on finer fabrics. Start just a centimetre into the seam, then back stitch to the end.

3 The foot plate is marked with different stitching guides. A standard seam allowance is 1.5cm.

HOW TO MAKE STRAIGHT SEAMS

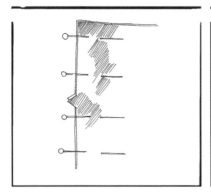

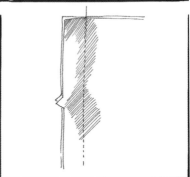

1 Matching up any notches, pin the seam together horizontally across the seam with the pin head on the seam edge side.

2 With presser foot up, slip the seam about 1cm under the foot and needle. Line up seam edge with foot-plate guide. Lower presser foot, stitch into the seam a few centimetres, then back stitch to secure. Using the foot-plate guide, stitch down the seam taking the pins out as you go. Finish the seam by back stitching.

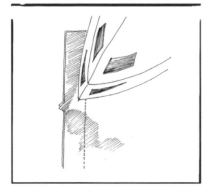
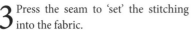

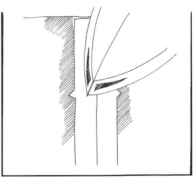

3 Press the seam to 'set' the stitching into the fabric.

4 Press the seam open in the same direction in which it was stitched.

TURNING A CORNER

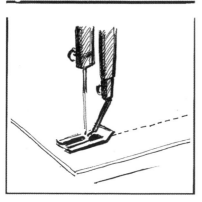

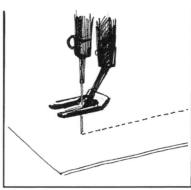

1 With the seam allowance lined up with the stitching guide, stitch towards the corner. Stop when the fabric reaches the cross-seam guide. Leave the needle down in the fabric.

2 With the needle still in the fabric, lift up the foot.

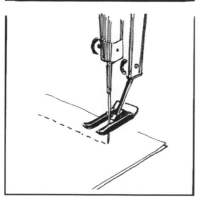

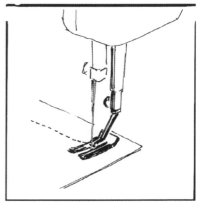

3 Turn the fabric to your required position and line up the start of the seam with the same stitching guide.

4 Lower the foot and start stitching your seam again.

STITCHING A CURVE

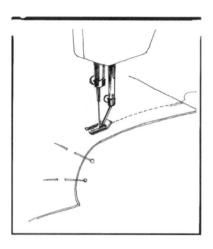

Particular care needs to be taken when stitching a curved seam to maintain an even seam allowance.

As the curve proceeds, the stitching guide may be obscured by the seam and only be visible right next to the foot. Use a smaller stitch for more control and stitch slowly.

WHEN SEAMS CROSS

When seams cross – at a waist seam, for example – they need to line up perfectly. Take time to align the seam carefully before you start sewing.

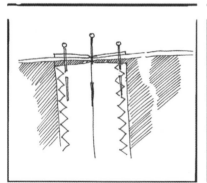

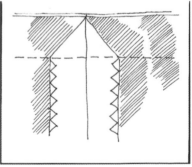

Line up both seams before stitching. Pin through the stitching line in both seams. Pin the seams open and flat.

Trim off the corners where the seams may cause bulk.

LINING UP SEAM ALLOWANCES

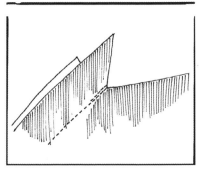
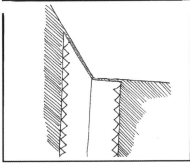

Seams can be cut at acute angles so that when they are pressed back they line up with the rest of the garment.

Line up the seams at the correct seam allowance.

UNDER STITCHING

Under stitching is an essential technique to ensure that facings sit in place inside the garment. This technique is used on both neck facing and armhole facings.

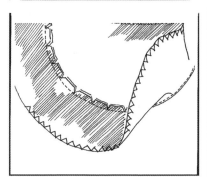
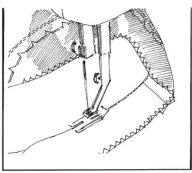

Under stitch on the right side of the facing close to the seam.

Stitch through the facing and the seam allowances only, not through to the right side of the garment.

NEATENING THE SEAM ALLOWANCE

ZIGZAG STITCH

The most common finish is a zigzag stitch. Most sewing machines will have this function.

Finishing all the seams will stop the seams fraying, so it is important for the longevity of the garment.

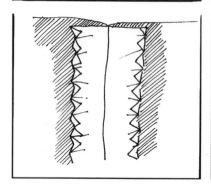

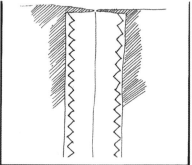

Plain straight seams are finished after the seam has been pressed open. Curved or cornered seams are finished directly after stitching; they are then clipped or notched.

Set the zigzag stitch to a medium width and short length. Stitch near the seam edge; do not zigzag right on the edge as this may distort or pucker the fabric.

This finish can be used on most fabrics, including knitted fabrics.

PINKED EDGE

Pinking shears are a quick and easy method to finish a seam, although they are suitable only for tightly woven light- to medium-weight fabrics such as crisp cottons.

Use the middle of the shear to cut. Realign each cut with the previous cut to keep a neatly pinked edge.

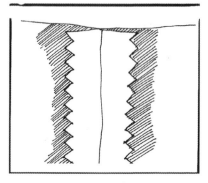

TOP STITCHING

Top stitching is done from the right side of the garment after the seams are finished and neatened, but before seams are joined to the next piece of the garment.

Check that the fabric top stitches well: some woollens, textured fabrics or fabrics with a nap may not be suitable for top stitching. Before starting, check that there is plenty of bobbin and top thread so there is no interruption in the stitching.

Avoid top stitching where there is no seam allowance behind.

As the stitching guide will not be visible when top stitching, the presser foot can be used as a guide to keep the stitching straight. Line up the side of the presser foot with the seam.

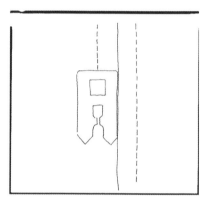

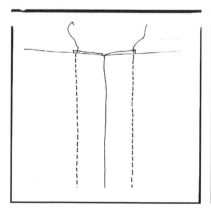

Top stitching can be done on either side of the seam through each seam allowance.

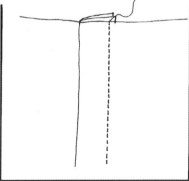

Top stitching done on one side should be through both seam allowances.

TRIMMING
SEAMS

Trimming seams is an important skill that will make all
the difference to the finish of a garment. Knowing when
and how to trim will help all the seams sit down perfectly.
Also take note of when and how to press a trimmed seam;
setting the seams in the right direction will make a
significant difference to the final garment. There are four
main methods to reduce bulk: trimming, layering, clipping
and notching.

TRIMMING

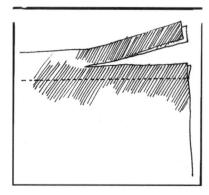

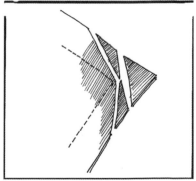

Trim down the seam when the full seam allowance gets in the way of fit, such as under the arm or in a construction such as a French seam. Trim down the seam allowance on both sides to make it smaller.

Trimming is used on an enclosed seam; pockets, corners and collar points should all be trimmed significantly to reduce bulk when they turn in on themselves.

LAYERING

Layering the seam allowance is done to reduce bulk on a seam that will be enclosed such as a collar facing. The widest part of the seam allowance should be on the front side of the garment, while the trimmed side should be on the inside of the garment. This graded or blended seam will be less bulky.

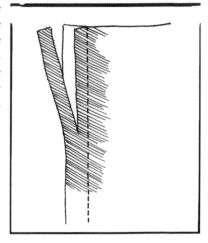

CLIPPING

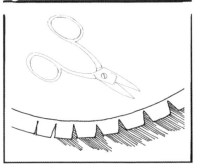

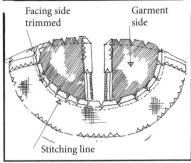

Facing side trimmed

Garment side

Stitching line

Clipping is used when the seam allowance needs to be spread to the same size as the garment, such as on a neck facing.

Clipping example: around a neck seam
The seam is layered and then clipped. Notice that the widest part of the seam is on the garment side.

NOTCHING

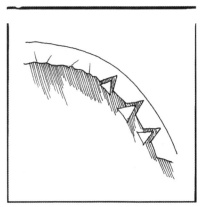

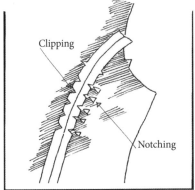

Clipping

Notching

Notching is used when the seam allowance is bigger than the garment allowance; the other side is concave and needs notching to reduce the excess in the seam allowance.

Notching example: Princess seam
Clipping is done to spread the seam allowance. Notching is done to reduce the excess fabric in the seam allowance.

HOW TO MAKE CORNERED SEAMS

To get a perfect corner for an item such as a collar or a cushion it is necessary to blunt the corner. This means that when you arrive at the corner, instead of turning straight away you take one stitch across the corner; you may need to take more stitches depending on the thickness of the fabric.

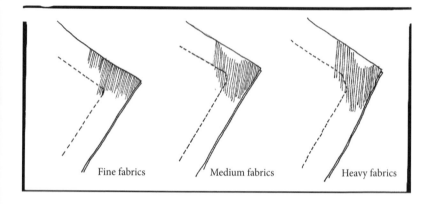

Fine fabrics   Medium fabrics   Heavy fabrics

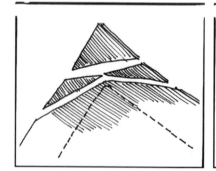

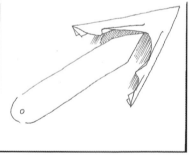

The seam is then clipped away to reduce the bulk.

All corners should be gently pushed out with a tool such as a point turner. Use a 'chewing' action rather than simply pushing. A large thick knitting needle can be used, but avoid using scissors as you may break through the seam.

INWARD CORNER

To make an inward corner fit to a straight seam it must be clipped to spread the seam.

The clipped corner will be vulnerable so it is reinforced with a line of stitching.

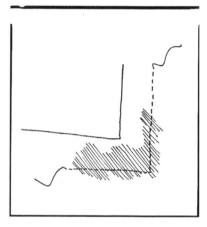

1 First stitch just inside the seam allowance and reinforce the corner with a line of stitching.

2 Clip into this corner; be careful not to cut into the stitching, but clip in as far as you can.

3 Spread the seam, pin into position and sew with the clipped side up.

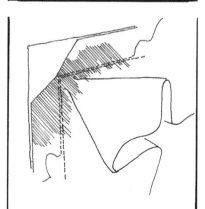

INTERFACING

Many patterns call for interfacing. Mostly this will be a fusible iron-on interfacing that has adhesive on one side. It is used where there is a need to define an area to help it hold its shape, such as collars, neck facings, cuffs and waistbands, or to reinforce the fabric in areas such as pockets, buttons and buttonholes. Interfacing always goes on the wrong side of the fabric and always on the facing, not on the garment.

CHOOSING INTERFACING

There are many different weights and types of interfacing for every possible type of fabric. Choosing the right one can be difficult; always go lighter rather than heavier, as the interfacing will become stiffer when the glue is melted on the fabric. Try to buy the interfacing at the same time as the fabric and ask for advice from the retailer.

Interfacing can be woven, non-woven or knit. Both knit and woven interfacings should be cut in the same direction as the pattern piece. Non-woven can be cut in any direction.

On pattern pieces, interfacing will be shaded differently on the pattern instructions and will be shown in the symbols key.

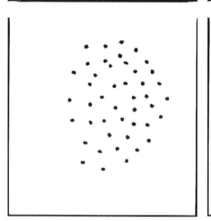

GUIDE TO INTERFACING WEIGHTS

FABRIC WEIGHT	INTERFACING WEIGHT
Lightweight and knitted fabrics	Sheer or feather-weight interfacing
Dress-weight fabrics	Lightweight interfacing
Suitings; medium- to heavy-weight fabrics	Medium-weight interfacing
Bags and accessories	Heavy-weight interfacing

USING FUSIBLE INTERFACING

1 Place the glued side down onto the wrong side of the fabric. Tip: It is wise to line up the fabric and interfacing with the pattern piece to make sure no distortion has occurred.

2 Use a medium-temperature dry iron. Tip: Interfacing is a delicate thing and can melt easily. For delicate fabrics, use a pressing cloth under the iron.

3 Hold the iron down for about 15 seconds, then lift and reposition. Repeat until the whole piece is fused perfectly. Tip: Press rather than iron so as not to distort the fabric.

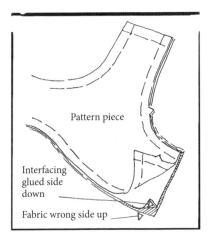

Pattern piece

Interfacing
glued side
down

Fabric wrong side up

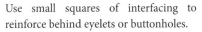

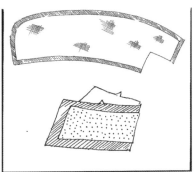

Use small squares of interfacing to reinforce behind eyelets or buttonholes.

Trim away the seam allowances from the interfacing to reduce bulk.

DARTS

Without darts we would need flat bodies in order for our clothes to fit nicely. Darts are simply a fold of fabric stitched to a point (like an actual dart) that creates contour shaping in a garment to accommodate rounded areas such as the bust or hips. The pattern piece seam allowance will be shaped so that when the dart is folded out and pressed in the correct direction it will sit back in the seam perfectly. Make sure you follow this shape when you are cutting out.

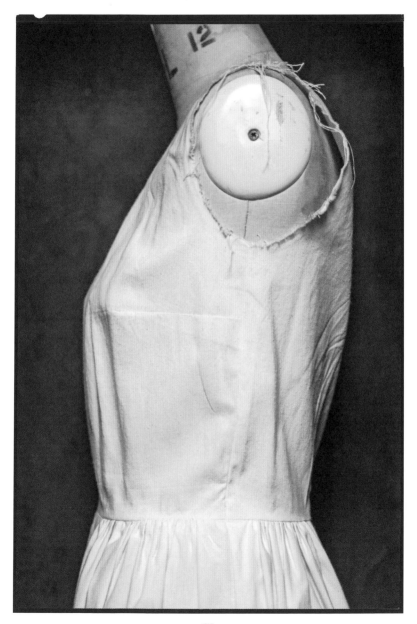

PLAIN DARTS

Darts are generally pressed towards the centre front or centre back or down towards the waist, as shown in the diagram below.

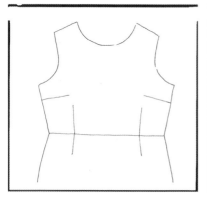

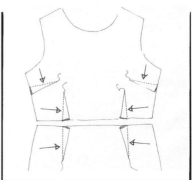

HOW TO MAKE PLAIN DARTS

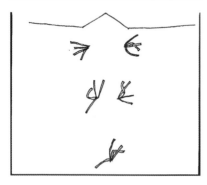

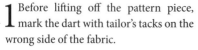

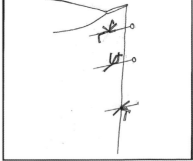

1 Before lifting off the pattern piece, mark the dart with tailor's tacks on the wrong side of the fabric.

2 With right sides together, fold out the dart matching up the tailor's tacks and pin together. Draw along the stitch line with tailor's chalk as a guide for sewing, or tack if preferred.

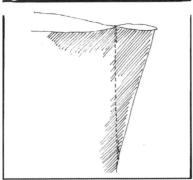

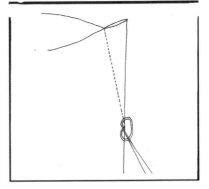

3 Starting from the top, stitch down to the point of the dart. Back stitch the beginning and the end of the dart, making sure to stay inside the stitch line.

4 On finer fabrics, leave long threads and tie into a knot at the end. Be careful not to tie too tight as this will pull the stitches. Remove all tailor's tacks.

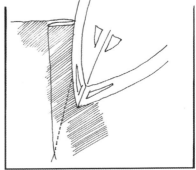

5 Press the stitching. Press the dart from either side; then, using a pressing cloth, press again on the right side.

6 Make sure that you only press the stitching so as to not let the dart fold show through to the front.

CONTOUR DARTS

Contour darts are long single darts that are widest in the middle and then taper off to a point at either end. They are generally found at the waistline to accommodate the fullness of the bust or the back and hips.

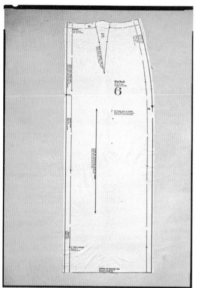
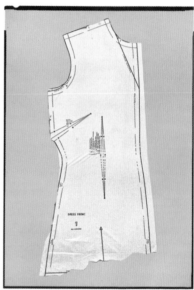

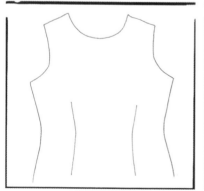

HOW TO MAKE CONTOUR DARTS

1 Before removing the pattern piece, mark the dart with tailor's tacks on the wrong side of the fabric.

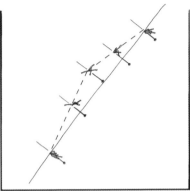

2 With the right sides together, fold out the dart and match up the tailor's tacks. Pin together, or tack if you prefer.

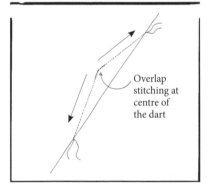

Overlap stitching at centre of the dart

3 Sew from the centre out to each point.

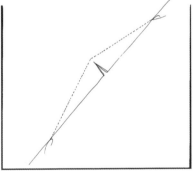

4 Secure with a back stitch. On finer fabrics, tie off the dart as for plain darts. Remove all the tacks. Snip the centre of the dart within 3mm of the stitching so that the dart will be free to curve smoothly. Press as for the plain dart.

SLEEVES

While we tend to pay most attention to the open end of a sleeve, in sewing the real action lies at the shoulder end. We will tackle three main types of sleeve. Each of these has a different look and fit and each employs a very different method of construction.

Set-in sleeves are the most traditional and common type of sleeve. Most set-in sleeves are cut to sit right on the shoulder. They give a flattering and tailored, fitted look.

Raglan sleeves have the seam cut across the body. They can be fitted or very loose. They give a comfortable look and indeed are comfortable to wear, allowing good freedom of movement.

Shirt sleeves have a casual look. They are often cut to have a dropped shoulder with the sleeve seam sitting slightly onto the arm. These sleeves are loose in fit.

We will also discuss finishing an armhole.

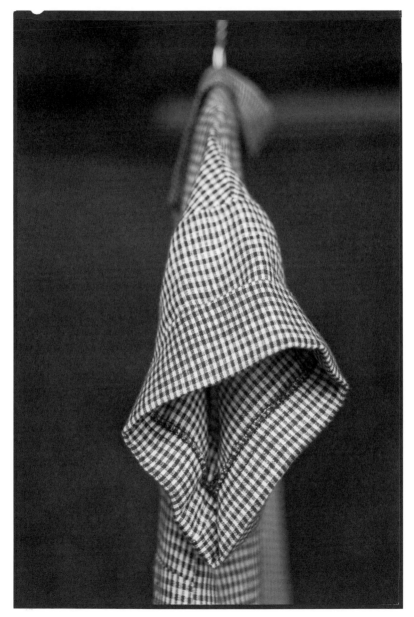

SET-IN SLEEVES

A set-in sleeve will have 'ease' at the sleeve head. It is called 'set in' because the shoulder and side seams of the garment are already sewn together and all seams pressed open and finished. This will give a lovely rounded line to the garment. Take care not to make any tucks in the sleeve when sewing in the sleeve. Ease is easiest to handle with loose-weave fabrics, such as woollens and linens, as it is easy to draw the fibres together; tightly woven fabrics such as denim are trickier.

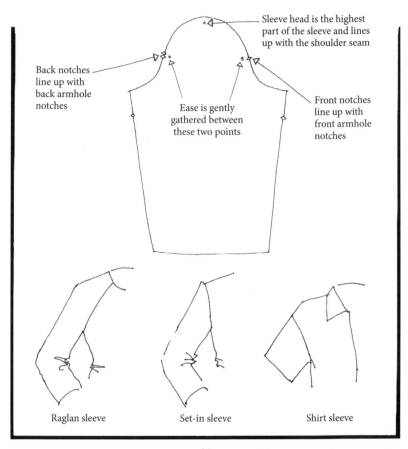

Sleeve head is the highest part of the sleeve and lines up with the shoulder seam

Back notches line up with back armhole notches

Ease is gently gathered between these two points

Front notches line up with front armhole notches

Raglan sleeve

Set-in sleeve

Shirt sleeve

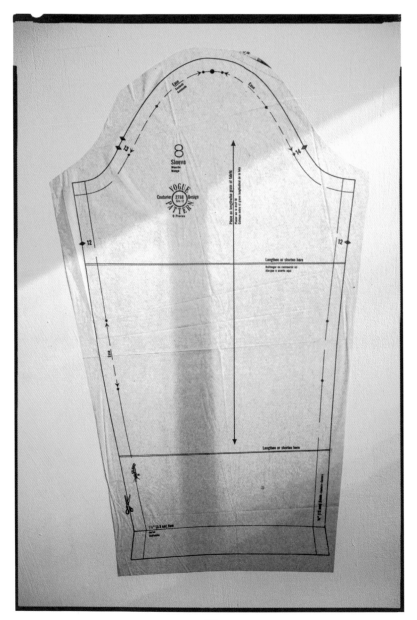

HOW TO SET IN SLEEVES

1 Join the sleeve seam, and ensure that you are making a pair.

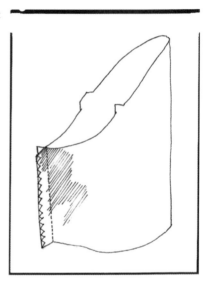

2 Using the largest stitch on the sewing machine, run a line of stitching between the front and back armhole notches, just inside the seam allowance. Secure one end with a back stitch and leave the other end with a long thread. Sewing in the other direction, sew another line of stitching parallel to the first, again securing one end with a back stitch and leaving the other end with a long thread. Turn the sleeve to the right side out. With the body of the garment inside out, drop the sleeve into the armhole.

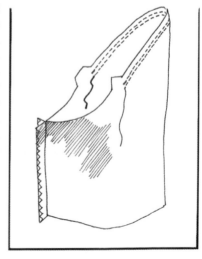

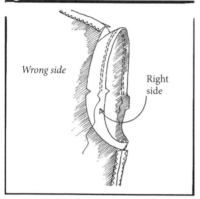

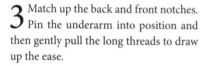

Wrong side

Right
side

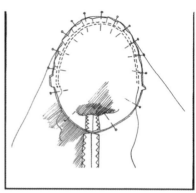

3 Match up the back and front notches. Pin the underarm into position and then gently pull the long threads to draw up the ease.

4 Even out the ease between the notches according to your pattern instructions. Pin into place, or tack if you prefer.

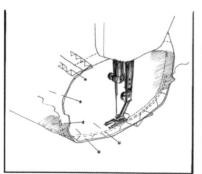

5 Sew the sleeve into place starting at the underarm seam and taking the pins out as you sew. Sew all the way around, making sure that the shoulder, sleeve and side seams are open and flat.

6 With the seam towards the sleeve (away from the body), zigzag the seams together.

RAGLAN SLEEVES

A raglan sleeve can be created as a two-piece sleeve, back and front, or with a dart to create a shoulder seam. The sleeve is 'set in'; that is, it is sewn into the body of the garment with the sleeve and the garment side seams sewn.

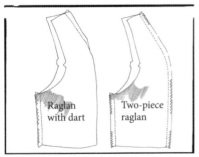

1 Either pin and create the dart or pin and sew the two-piece sleeve together. Make sure that you are creating a pair of sleeves, and press the seams open.

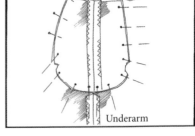

2 Sew together the underarm seam on both the sleeve and the garment body. With right sides together, pin the sleeve to the body of the garment, matching the underarm seams and matching the notches.

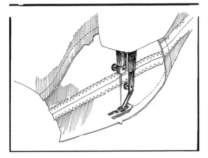

3 With the sleeve side up, carefully sew into place.

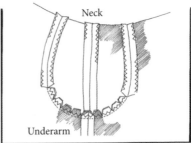

4 Press the seam open from both sides of the fabric. Clip seams at front and back notches to allow seams at the neck to lie open. Zigzag underarm seams together. Zigzag other seams individually.

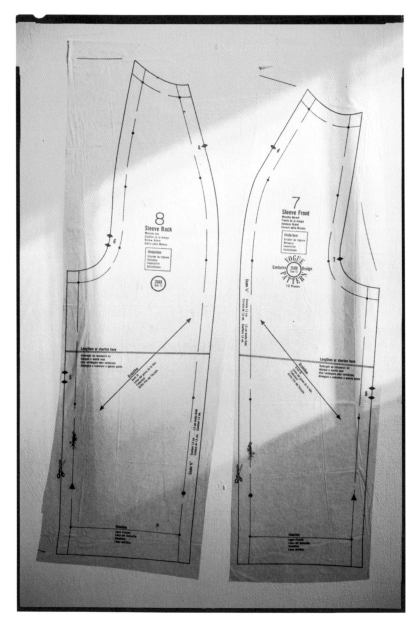

SHIRT SLEEVES

This style of sleeve offers a more casual look, as it is a looser fit and can be dropped away from the natural shoulder.

There is normally no ease allowance in a shirt sleeve. It is put in on the flat before the side and sleeve seams are sewn.

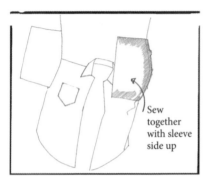

Sew together with sleeve side up

1 With right sides together, pin the sleeve into the armholes, matching the notches as you go. Sew together with sleeve side up.

2 Press the seam open, then press the seam towards the sleeve (away from the body). Zigzag the sleeve and armhole seams together to finish the seam.

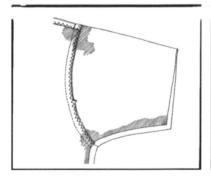

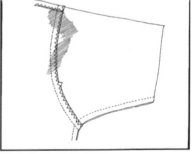

3 Matching up the underarm seams, pin and sew the side seams and the sleeve seams together. Start sewing from the side seam, then sew down the sleeve seam.

4 Press the seam open and finish each of the seams with a zigzag.

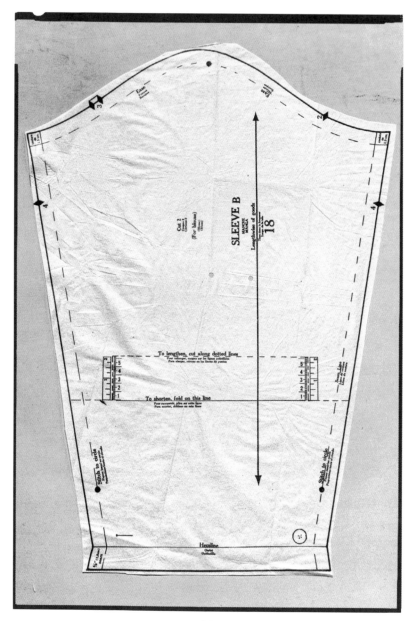

FINISHING AN ARMHOLE

There are several methods of finishing an armhole. We will look at two of them here. The first is a very simple basic faced armhole that, once finished, can be held in place with a cross stitch at the shoulder and the underarm. For a more professional finish, we also look at making a fully faced armhole and neck. This is more complicated to achieve but gives a great result.

USING A BASIC FACING

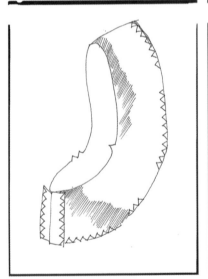

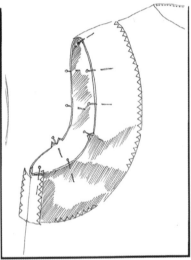

1 Join the underarm seams of the facing and press the seam open. Finish the outside edge of the facing with a zigzag.

2 With the garment right side out and the facing wrong side out (so that right sides are together), pin the facing to the armhole. Match the underarm seams and all the armhole notches. Make sure all seams are open and flat.

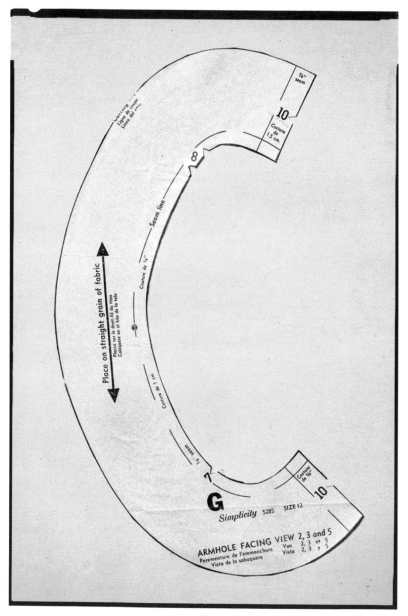

Place on straight grain of fabric
Placez sur le droit-fil du tissu
Colóquese en el hilo de la tela

Cutting line
Ligne de Coupe
Línea del corte

Seam line

5/8" seam

Couture de 1.5 cm.

Couture de 5/8"

Couture de 1 cm.

5/8" seam

Couture de 5/8"

10

8

7

10

G

Simplicity 5285   SIZE 12

ARMHOLE FACING VIEW 2, 3 and 5
Parementure de l'emmanchure   Vue   2, 3 et 5
Vista de la sobaquera   Vista   2, 3 y 5

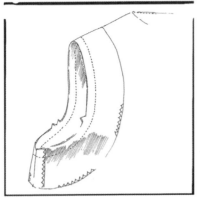

3 Starting at the underarm, stitch around the whole armhole.

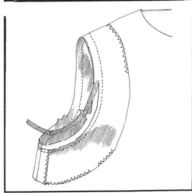

4 Trim down the facing seam only, leaving the garment side as it is.

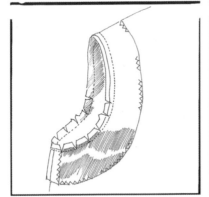

5 Snip around the underarm between back and front notches.

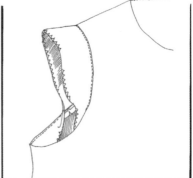

6 Press the seam open, then press again towards the facing. Under stitch through the seam allowances only, close to the seam (see step 7 page 116). Turn the facing to the inside and press from inside.

USING A FULL FACING

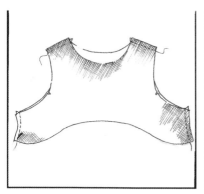

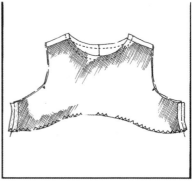

1 Pin and stitch the shoulder seams together. Press the seams open. Pin and stitch the side seams together. Finish the seams and press open. Finish the bottom with zigzag or overlock.

2 With the garment the right side out and the facing inside out (right sides are facing each other), pin and stitch the facing to the neck of the garment. Trim the seams, press and under stitch following steps 3–7 of neck facings (pages 114–116). Turn the facing to the inside of the garment.

3 On the inside of the garment, place pins at point **a** (top of the underarm seam) and point **b** (bottom of the underarm seam).

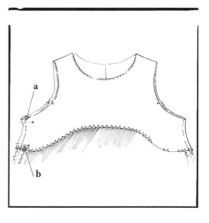

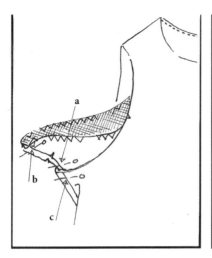

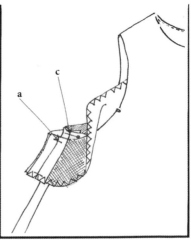

4 Lift the facing out of the armhole, flipping it over so that pin **a** and pin **c** are facing each other.

5 The right sides of the garment and facing are now together.

6 With all seams open, start pinning the facing armhole to the garment armhole. The armhole will feel twisted and odd.

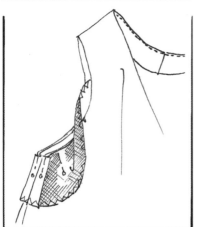

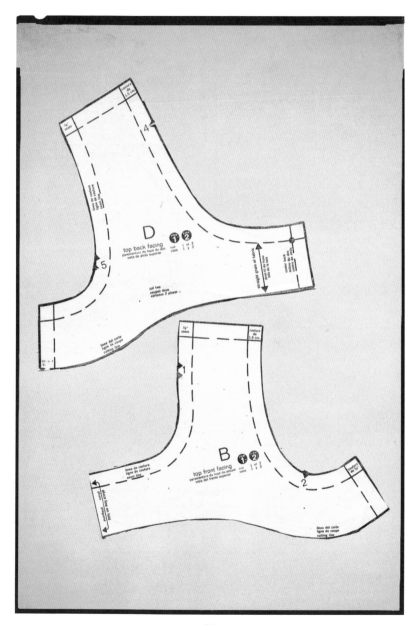

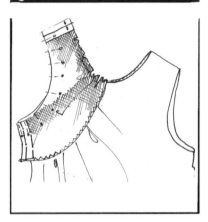

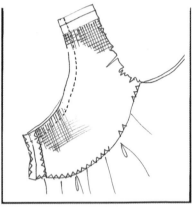

7 Continue to pin around the armhole, pulling the facing through until just past the shoulder seam.

8 One side at a time, stitch from the underarm to just beyond the shoulder seam. Repeat for the other side.

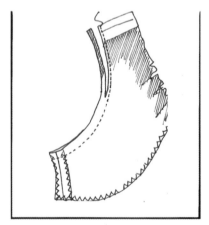

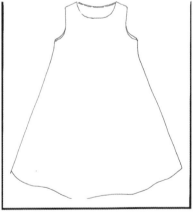

9 Trim down and snip the seams between the back and front armhole notches.

10 Turn through to the right side and press well from both sides.

WAISTLINES

The waistline is a pivot point for a dress and a finishing line for trousers or a skirt. Often overlooked, this line draws the eye and so the finish and attention to detail is important. The way in which the waistline conceals underlying fabric, from below or above, means that these joins must be finished neatly and smoothly to avoid bulk or lumps. When pressing, a waist seam is always pressed up towards the bodice.

In this chapter, we look at constructing a gathered waist seam and a darted waist seam and include the simplest way to achieve a good functional waistband for trousers, shorts and skirts.

JOINING A BODICE TO A SKIRT

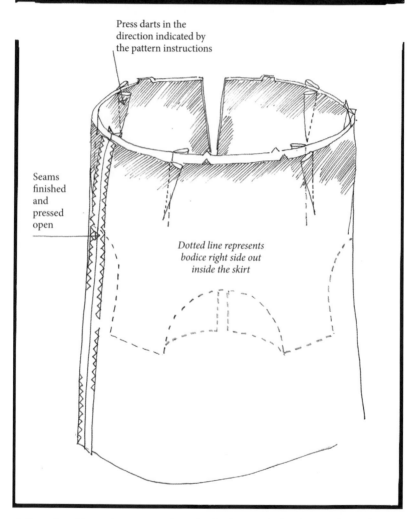

Press darts in the direction indicated by the pattern instructions

Seams finished and pressed open

Dotted line represents bodice right side out inside the skirt

1 Turn the skirt to the wrong side and the bodice to the right side. Slip the bodice inside the skirt so that right sides are together.

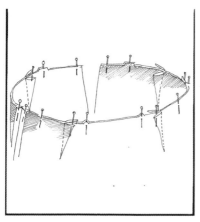

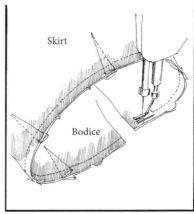

2 Carefully match and pin into place all side seams, darts and notches.

3 Stitch the waist seam, starting and finishing at the zip opening. You will find that it is easier to stitch from the inside.

4 Press the seam flat and finish the seam by zigzagging the seam together. Press the seam up towards the bodice. Pull the bodice out of the skirt and press the seam again.

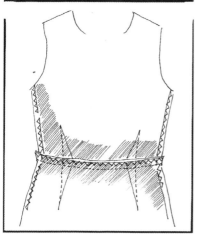

HOW TO GATHER

1 On each section of the garment, using the largest stich on the sewing machine, sew two parallel lines inside the seam allowance. Do not sew over the seams as these will not gather well, but do make sure that the stitches go right up to the seams or there will be a gap in the gathering. Leave long threads at both ends.

2 Pin the bodice and skirt together matching up all the notches and side seams. If there is a zip that intersects the waist seam this will be set in after the waist seam is finished.

With bodice right way out and skirt inside out, slip the bodice inside the skirt so that right sides are together

Dotted line indicates bodice inside the skirt

All side seams should be finished

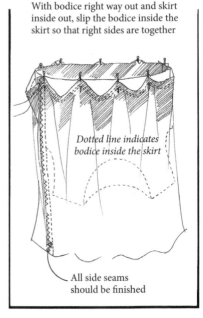

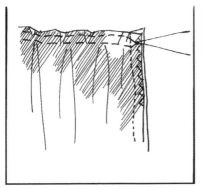

3 Tie off the threads on one side, leaving the other side free.

4 Pull up the threads on the free side to gather, then fit, pin into place and tie off. Repeat between the seams on all sections. Pin the seam allowances open.

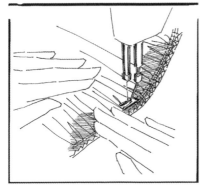

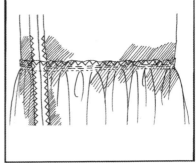

5 With the gathering right side up, sew into place. Hold the fabric tight on either side to prevent small tucks forming in the gathers.

6 Press the stitching only, leaving the gathers free. Finish the seam by zigzagging both seam allowances together. The final seam should sit upwards away from the gathers.

ATTACHING A WAISTBAND

1 First, iron on a fusible interfacing to the wrong side on half of the waistband. Press up the seam allowance on the other side.

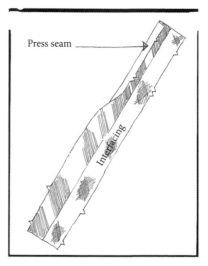

Press seam

Interfacing

2 With right sides together and matching any notches, pin the waistband with the interfaced section to the body of the garment so that when the waistband is finished the interfacing side will be on the front. Stitch the waistband into place. Trim down the seams.

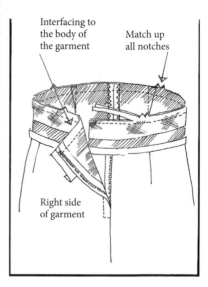

Interfacing to the body of the garment

Match up all notches

Right side of garment

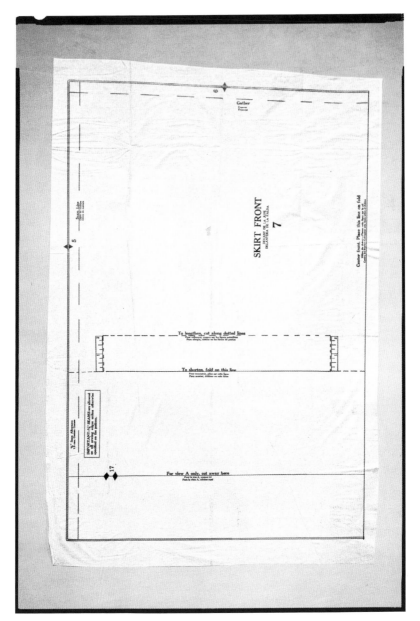

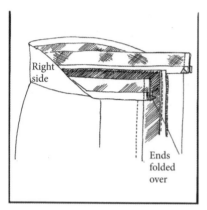

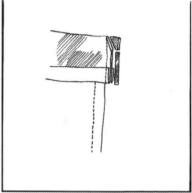

3 Turn over each end of the waistband so that the right sides are together. Stitch into place.

4 Trim off the corners and trim down the seams.

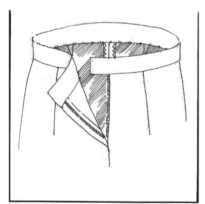

5 Turn through to the right side and slip stitch the inside of the waistband into place.

6 The button sits on the inside on the facing extension and the buttonhole is on the top.

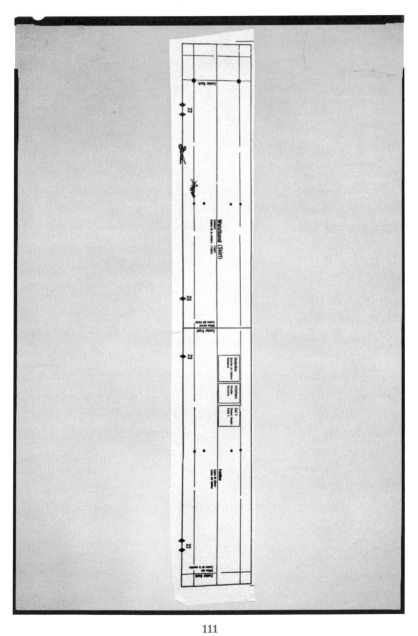

NECKLINES

The key to achieving a successful neckline lies in the trimming, pressing and under stitching. It is important to understand these skills.

A garment, and its quality of finish, may stand or fall by the neckline, which, after all, is right on show at the front. Continuing in the spirit of achievable, effective techniques, in this chapter we look at a simple faced neckline and two types of collar: a flat collar (sometimes called a Peter Pan collar) and a one-piece rolled collar.

All three methods require a facing (usually interfaced for stability), which is used to conceal the raw edges of the neckline and the front and back openings. Both the simple neck facing and the Peter Pan collar follow the same method and can be made with or without a front or back opening. They are the simplest necklines to achieve.

The rolled collar has a built-in collar stand that rises up onto the neck. It is important to centre the collar and facing; stitch from the centre back out towards the centre front to avoid stretching the fabric in opposite directions.

SIMPLE FACED NECKLINE

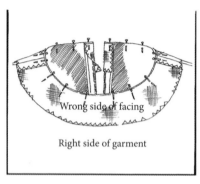

Wrong side of facing

Right side of garment

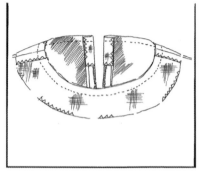

1 With the garment the right side out, pin the neck facing to the neck so that the right sides are together. Line up all the notches. Open the zip and wrap the ends of the neck facing around each side of the zip.

2 With the facing side up, stitch around the neck. Stitch over the zip opening, making sure that the neck seam lines up when the zip is closed. Press the seam flat to set the stitching.

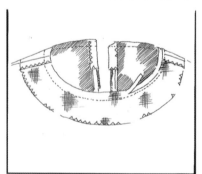

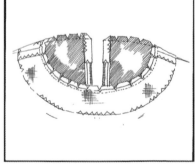

3 Layer the seam allowance by trimming the facing seam only.

4 Clip the seam and trim the corners of the zip opening.

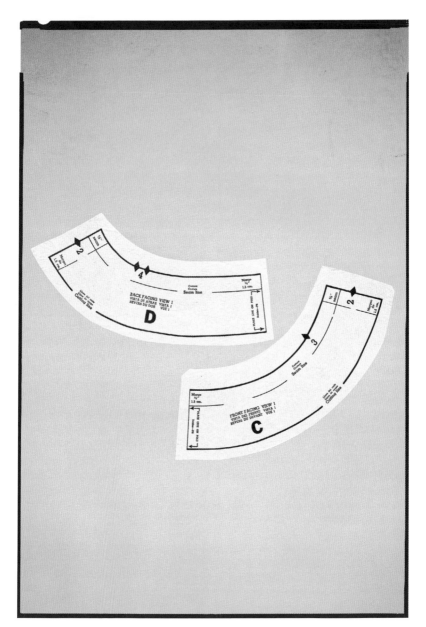

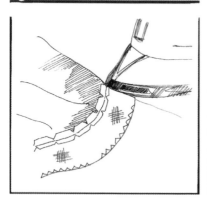

5 Press the seam open.

6 Press the seam closed up towards the facing.

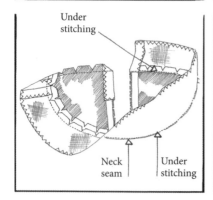

Under
stitching

Neck
seam

Under
stitching

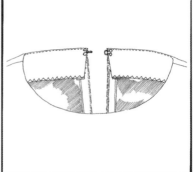

7 Under stitch the facing seam to help the facing sit on the inside of the garment. Edge stitch close to the seam through the facing and garment seams only. Press the facing well from the inside of the garment.

8 Fold the ends of the neck facing under and slip stich into place, making sure that the zip can run freely without getting caught in the seam. Finish the top of the zip with a hook and eye.

DIFFERENT TYPES OF NECKLINES

Flat collar

Neck facing

One-piece collar

FLAT COLLAR (PETER PAN COLLAR)

A Peter Pan collar sits flat and is only decorative. It can be made of two separate sides or one whole piece. In each case there is an underside and a top side of the collar. The underside is interfaced and will be slightly smaller to allow the edge seam to roll towards the under collar.

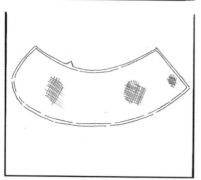

1 Iron on fusible interfacing to the wrong side of each underside collar piece.

2 Stitch the top and bottom collar pieces along their outer edge.

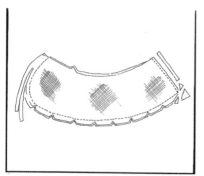

3 Trim down the back seam and corners, layer and notch the seam.

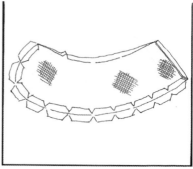

4 Press the seam open.

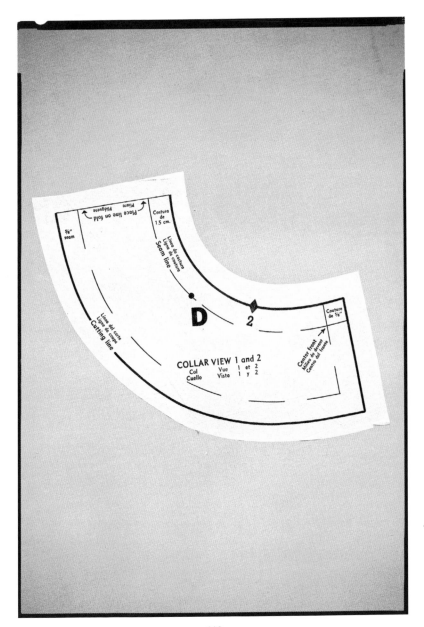

COLLAR VIEW 1 and 2
Col   Vue   1 et 2
Cuella   Vista   1 y 2

D   2

Place line on fold
Pliure
5/8" seam
Costura de 1.5 cm.
Línea de costura
Ligne de couture
Seam line

Línea del corte
Ligne de coupe
Cutting line

Couture de 5/8"

Center Front
Milieu de Devant
Centro del Frente

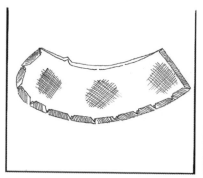 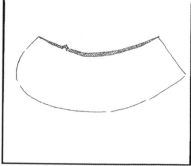

5 Press the seams towards the underside.

6 Turn the collar piece through to the right side. The top piece is slightly bigger than the underside. Press so that the seam sits slightly towards the underside.

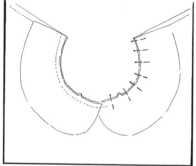 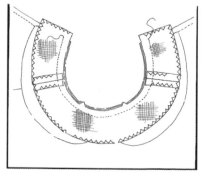

7 Pin the collar pieces to the neckline matching neckline notches. The front piece should overlap on the neckline but should meet perfectly on the stitching line. Stitch into position.

8 With right sides together, pin and stitch the neck facing over the collar (this should be interfaced and finished on the outer edge).

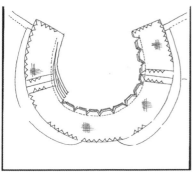

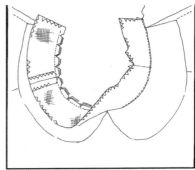

9 Layer the neck seam and notch. Press the seam open and then press the seam away from the neck.

10 Under stitch (see page 65 for details)

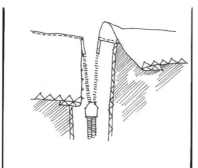

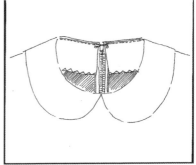

11 Fold the facing to the inside of the neck and press. Fold the ends of the facing in under the facing and slip stitch into place.

12 Sew on a hook and eye to finish the closing if needed.

ONE-PIECE FLAT COLLAR

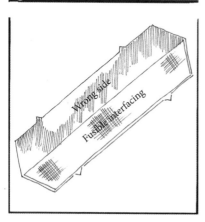

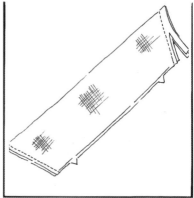

1 Turn the collar piece to the wrong side. Iron on the fusible interfacing to one side of the collar piece.

2 Fold the collar over on itself and stitch down the ends, back stitching the beginning and end of the seam to secure. Layer the seams, making the interfaced side the narrower seam. Trim the corners.

3 Press the seams open. Turn through to the right side. Using a pressing cloth, press the collar well.

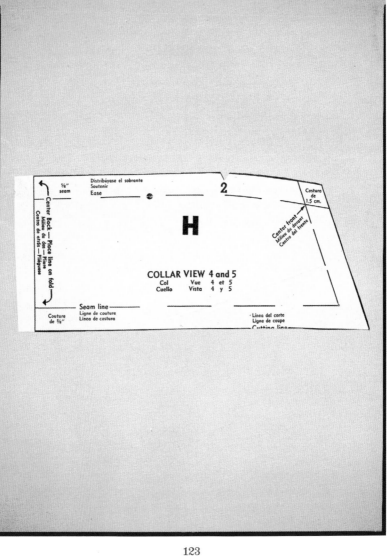

H

COLLAR VIEW 4 and 5
Col   Vue   4 et 5
Cuello   Vista   4 y 5

⅝″ seam

Distribúyase el sobrante
Soutenir
Ease

Costura de 1.5 cm.

Center Back — Place line on fold
Milieu du dos — Pliure
Centro de atrás — Pliéguese

Center front
Milieu du devant
Centro del frente

Seam line
Ligne de couture
Línea de costura

Couture de ⅝″

Línea del corte
Ligne de coupe
Cutting line

2

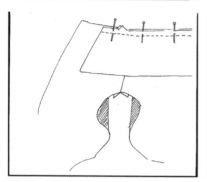 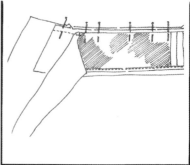

4 Pin the collar to the garment body with the interfaced side to the body of the garment. Match up the notches, snipping into the collar seam to help it fit the neckline if necessary. Starting from the centre back, stitch just inside the seam allowance to each end of the collar.

5 Create the facing and finish its outside raw edge. Pin over the collar, matching up all notches.

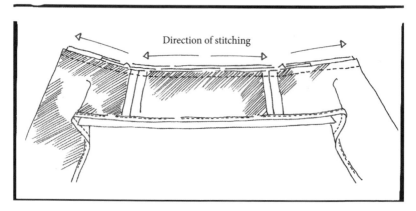

Direction of stitching

6 Starting at the centre back, stitch just inside the seam allowance right to each end of the facing. This will hold the collar and facing in place.

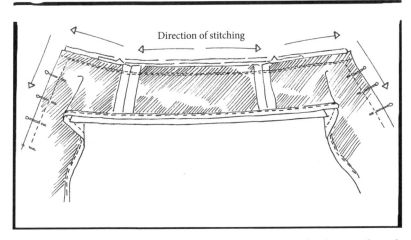

Direction of stitching

7 Again starting at the centre back, stitch on the seam allowance along the neck pivot at the front and stitch down the centre front seams.

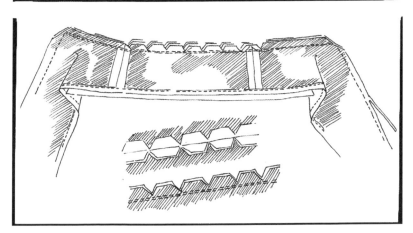

8 Notch into the back neck through all seams. Trim the front seams. Press all the seams open, then press up towards the collar.

TROUSERS

To make trousers, we are in essence uniting a pair of mirror-image legs at the gusset. It sounds easy enough but, as ever, there is a simple technique that will save time and perspiration, especially if we dip into the world of zips and crotch fastenings.

JOINING TROUSERS

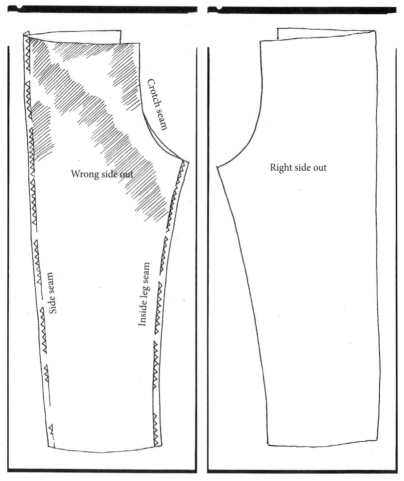

1 Join the side and inside leg seams. Press the seams open and finish with a zigzag stitch.

2 Turn one leg through to the right side leaving the other leg inside out.

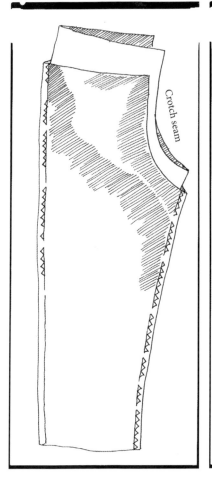

Crotch seam

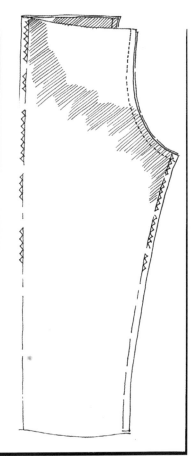

3 Slip the right-side-out leg inside the other leg so that right sides are together. Match up the inside leg seams and pin the seam allowances open. Match up any crotch notches.

4 Pin together and stitch around the curve of the crotch seam.

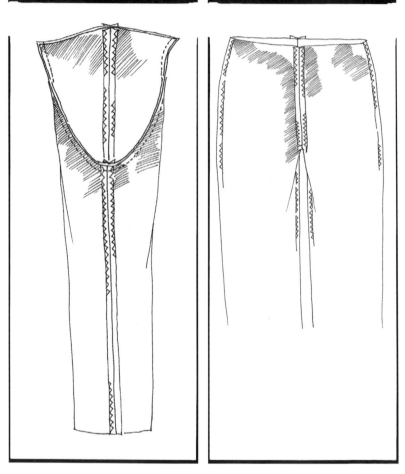

5 Pull one trouser leg out of the other.

6 Press the seam open and finish the seam with a zigzag.

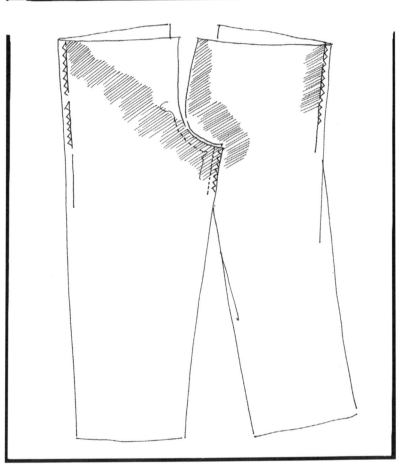

7 If there is a front zip fastening, the pattern may instruct you to stitch only part of the crotch seam. This means you will be able to insert the zip on the flat, which is a much easier method.

POCKETS

To keep it simple, it is tempting to make up a garment without pockets. Nevertheless, pockets are useful and make a great feature as well as making a garment look and feel more comfortable.

In-seam pockets are the easiest to accomplish. Their success (or not) depends on the correct direction of the seams and the accurate snipping of the seams so that everything lies flat and neat.

Patch pockets are charming, yet can be difficult to achieve as they require attentive top stitching that needs to be very neat and can be unforgiving. Before attempting a patch pocket, check that the fabric can take a tidy top stitch, remembering to choose the right colour thread – especially on a patterned fabric. The wrong choice can make the pocket look amateur and be somewhat disheartening to behold.

IN-SEAM POCKETS

The neatest way to create an in-seam pocket is with an all-in-one pocket on the side seam. However, this can take a lot of extra fabric, so a pocket extension is a good alternative. The method for the all-in-one-pocket is the same.

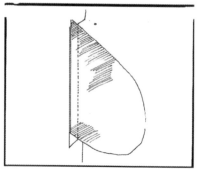

1 With right sides together, sew all pockets onto the pocket extensions.

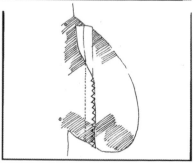

2 Press seams open, then press towards the pocket. Zigzag seams together.

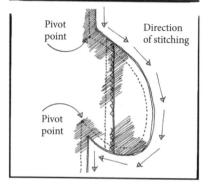

3 Pin the side seams together, pinning around the pockets. Sew down the seam to the pivot point, turn and sew around the pockets to the other pivot point, then turn and sew down the seam.

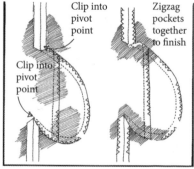

4 Clip the seam at the top and bottom of the pockets to allow the seams to be pressed open and finished. Zigzag around the pockets, sewing both pockets together.

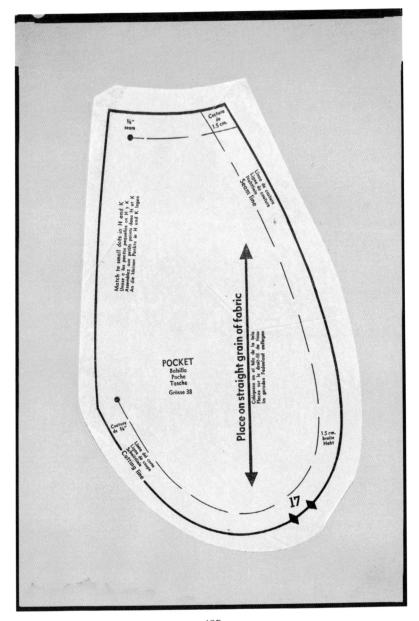

PATCH POCKETS

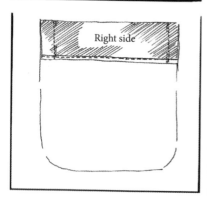

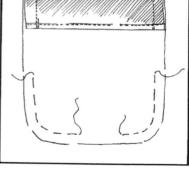

1 Turn over the top edge and stitch down. Fold over the facing to the right side and stitch into place, then back stitch to secure.

2 Using the largest stitch on the sewing machine, run two lines of ease stitching around the corners of the pocket just inside the seam allowance.

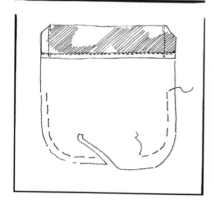

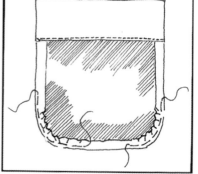

3 Trim the corners and trim down the outside seam. Turn through the facing to the wrong side, poking out the corners.

4 Press up the seam allowance. Gently draw up the ease stitches to make a neat curve. Press all around the edge of the pocket.

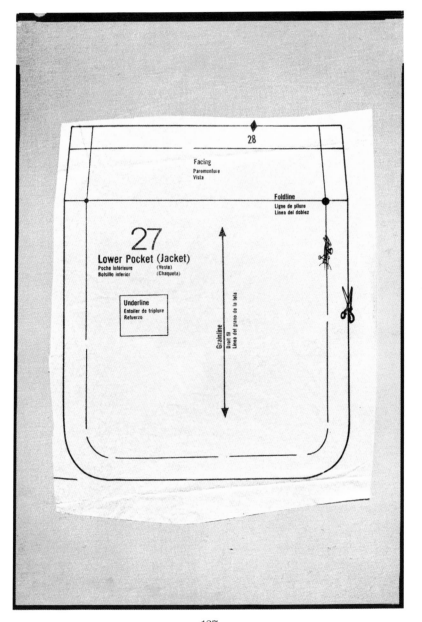

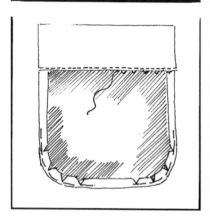

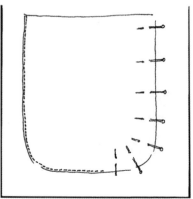

5 Notch the seams to remove the excess seam allowance, then slip stitch the pocket turning into place. Using a pressing cloth, press from the front.

6 Line up the pocket with the position markings on the garment. Pin into place. Stitch as close as possible to the edge of the pocket, taking out the pins just before sewing over them.

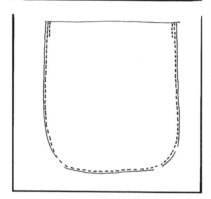

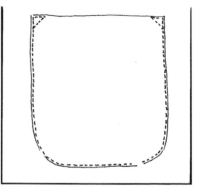

7 Reinforce the corners of the pocket either with a back stitch (above left) or with two evenly sized triangles (above right).

ZIPS

The humble zip, ingenious, absurdly useful yet often hidden, can strike fear into the sewing beginner. Following some simple principles and basic techniques will have you perfectly zipped up in no time. You will need to use a zipper foot – it has notches in the sides and can be moved from left to right, allowing you to stitch close to the zip teeth.

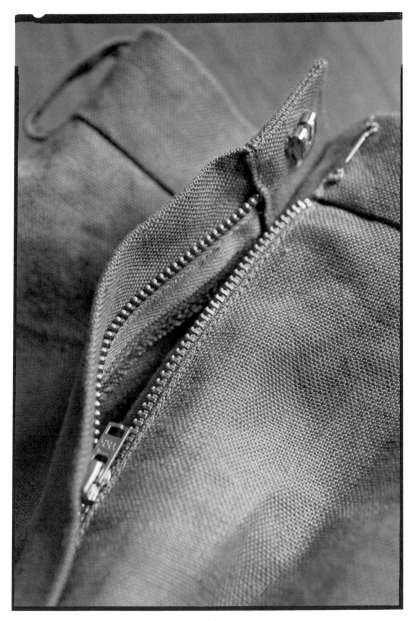

SEMI-CONCEALED ZIP

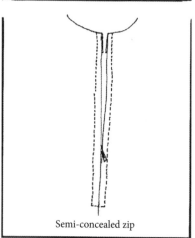

Semi-concealed zip

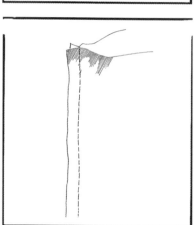

1 Using the standard sewing machine foot, sew the seam together up to the zip opening notch. Change the stitch length to the largest stitch and sew up the remainder of the seam. Press the seam open.

2 Change to the zipper foot. Place the closed zip face down onto the closed seam, aligning the centre of the zip to the seam.

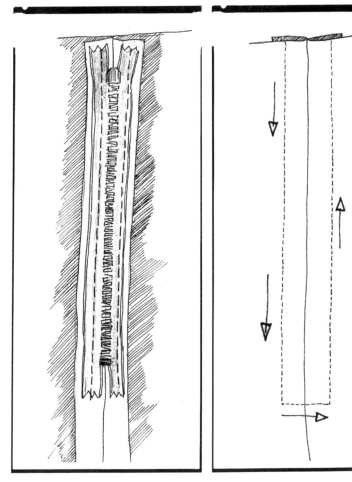

3 Sew each side of the zip into place, sewing through the seam allowance only. This is just to hold the zip in place.

4 Turn to the front and top stitch into place as shown. Using an unpicker, open up the seam with the large stitching.

CONCEALED LAPPED ZIP

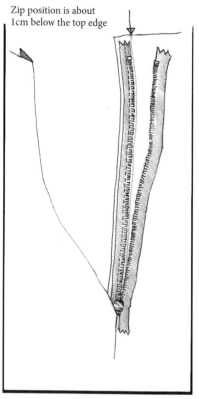

Zip position is about
1cm below the top edge

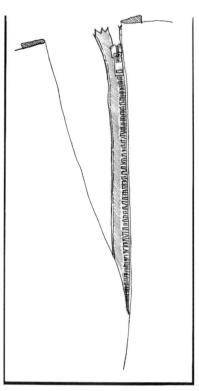

1 Sew up the seam to the notch that marks the beginning of the zip opening. Press the seam open all the way to the top. Place the open zip face down onto the face of the fabric. Slip the zip end between the seams. The zip teeth need to be exactly on the centre of the seam. Sew down the zip as close as you can to the teeth seam.

2 Turn to the right side and make sure that the opposite seam will lap over the top nicely.

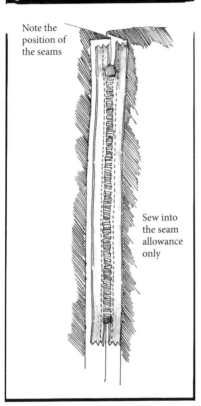

Note the position of the seams

Sew into the seam allowance only

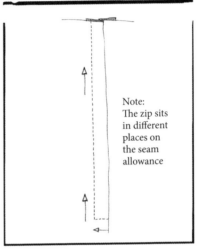

Note: The zip sits in different places on the seam allowance

4 Top stitch the front of the zip, starting at the bottom. Sew across the bottom, lift the foot (keeping the needle in place), turn the cloth, put the foot down again and sew to the top.

3 Turn to the wrong side again and sew the other side of the zip into the seam allowance only, not through to the front. Turn to the front. If necessary, tack the lapped seam closed to stabilize the seam. Unpick the tacking afterwards.

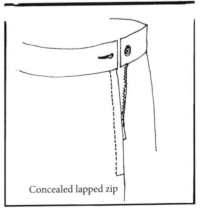

Concealed lapped zip

BUTTONHOLES

Buttonholes are not difficult to make, but they can be the crowning glory to a garment and a testament to your skills, so treat them with care. There are different methods for making buttonholes, from hand-finished to computer-programmed. The technique we cover here is the most common and, luckily, the easiest: a machined buttonhole. All modern sewing machines have a buttonhole function, which should not be hard to master.

A machined buttonhole is a slit in the fabric flanked by two equal-length sides of short, tightly spaced zigzag stitches. It is stitched through the garment, and the facing where applicable, and each end is finished with a bar tack – a wider zigzag top and bottom. The opening in the buttonhole is only cut after stitching; you can use an unpicker or buttonhole scissors, which are sharp to the very tips and made for the job.

When working with pattern pieces, use chalk or tailor's tacks to transfer the marks for buttonhole positions from the pattern. Take care when making up the garment not to lose any of these markings.

If in doubt, make a test buttonhole on a spare piece of fabric before risking your new garment – unpicking a buttonhole is not ideal, as the heavy stitching will damage the fabric.

BUTTONHOLE MARKINGS ON A PATTERN

➤ Note: Interfacing should always be used where a buttonhole is to be sewn to strengthen the area and hold the stitches.

➤ Buttonholes on women's garments are placed on the right-hand side on garments that fasten on the front and on the left-hand side if they fasten at the back.

➤ Horizontal buttonholes are the most secure, while vertical buttonholes are often used on shirts when there are many small buttons.

➤ The button position will be at least three-quarters of the size of the button away from the garment edge.

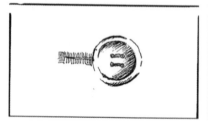

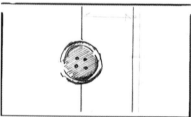

Buttonholes can be either vertical or horizontal on the garment.

Buttons are sewn onto the centre front line. This means the buttonhole is set off-centre to the centre front line so the button will sit at the end of the buttonhole when the garment is closed.

HOW TO MARK BUTTONHOLES

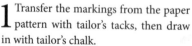

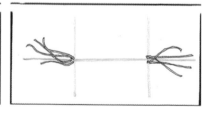

1 Transfer the markings from the paper pattern with tailor's tacks, then draw in with tailor's chalk.

2 Draw long lines that cross so that when machining the buttonhole the marks can be seen on either side of the foot.

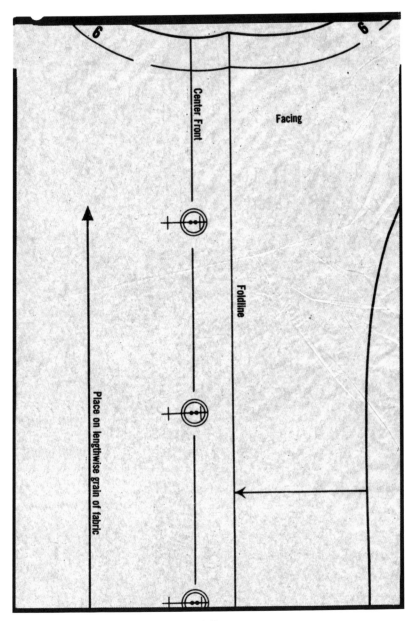

WORKING OUT BUTTONHOLE SIZE

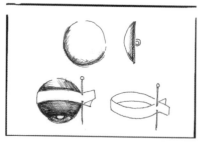

MACHINING A BUTTONHOLE

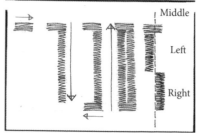

Work out the measurements for drawing the buttonhole size as follows: diameter + height + 3mm.

For a ball button: pin a strip of pattern around the ball button, then measure the paper to find the buttonhole length.

Most sewing machines will be able to sew a buttonhole. Depending on the machine, this may be automatic or semi-manual.

THE BUTTONHOLE FEATURE

CUTTING OPEN BUTTONHOLES

This feature allows the needle position to move so that it can sew in the middle for the bar tack; to the right for one side of the buttonhole; and to the left for the other side of the buttonhole.

Machine-worked buttonholes are cut after they have been sewn. Put in a pin at either end to prevent cutting through the stitches. Use a sharp but strong pair of scissors to cut with special care down the centre of the buttonhole.

BUTTON POSITION

SEWING ON A BUTTON FLAT TO THE GARMENT

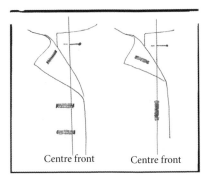

Centre front   Centre front

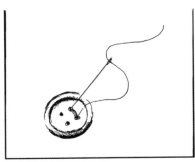

To check the button position, lap the buttonhole sections over each other and line up the centre fronts, top and bottom. Push a pin through the buttonhole 3mm from the end of the buttonhole; this will give you the perfect button position.

Secure the thread by sewing a few stitches on the button position mark. Then centre the button over this and sew in place through the holes. Secure the thread on the wrong side.

SEWING ON A BUTTON WITH A THREAD SHANK

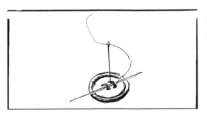

1 Make a shank to allow the button to pass through thicker fabrics and still sit flat. Secure the thread at the button position mark and pass the needle through one of the holes. Then place a needle on top of the button and stitch over the needle and through the holes.

2 Make about six stiches, then remove the pin and pull up the button away from the fabric to create the shank. Wind the thread tightly around the shank, secure the thread, and back stitch through the shank.

HEMS

Simply put, a hem is a folded, finished end line to a garment that conceals raw fabric edges and assorted unsightly joins. Skirts, sleeves, trouser legs and jackets all sport hemming techniques that, if made well enough, will never be noticed. Be aware that your hem might be the most visible part of the garment – a waistband may be perfect, but will not be so open to scrutiny. For a truly professional finish, carefully press just your hem edge and take your time.

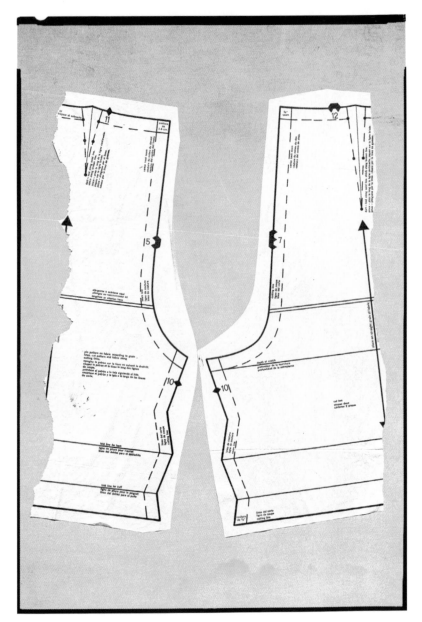

A NOTE ON HEMS

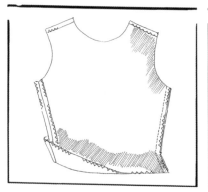

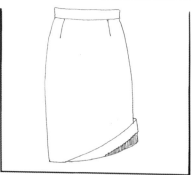

Some pattern pieces are cut so that the folded hem will fit perfectly in the finished position. Should you then need to shorten or lengthen your garment, use the indications on the pattern rather than simply lopping off cloth at the hem.

A straight shape can accommodate a deep hem of 5–7cm.

A fuller or flared shape requires a narrower hem of about 3cm; even then, the hem may need to be eased in.

A top-stitched hem can be quite narrow, at 1.5–2cm, and gives an intrinsically more casual look.

THE PERFECT HEM

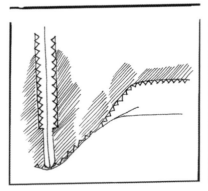

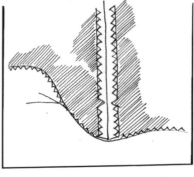

Before starting your hem, either trim down the seam or cut a small notch into the seam to mark the point where it will fold up.

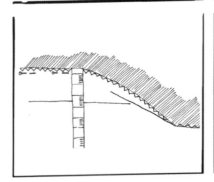

Turn up the hem, using a tape measure to keep it even. Pin the hem into position and press at the edge only to hold in place.

The neatest stitch to use on a hem is a blind hemming stitch, which works like slip stitch. The stitch is taken *inside* – between the garment and the hem. Keeping the join prised open, use the needle tip to pick up the fibres rather than grabbing the whole thickness of the cloth. You will be rewarded with an invisible finish, as the hem cannot press into the garment.

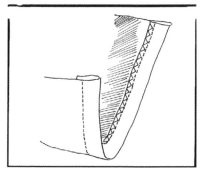

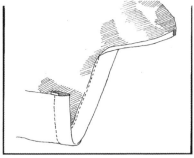

A simple top-stitched hem is finished with a zigzag, pressed over and top stitched from the right side of the garment. Always press the hem after stitching.

For a more refined finish, turn over the hem once, by about 0.5cm, and press. Then turn over again so that no edges are visible. Note that some thicker fabrics are too bulky for this method.

Thick paper between the hem and the garment

Before turning up the hem, run a line of small tacking stitches along the edge that will become your hem. Turn up the hem, pulling up the tacking stitches so the hem fits neatly. Press into position using thick paper in between the hem and the garment to avoid marking the front.

All hems need pressing well. Press only along the hem edge to avoid the turn showing through onto the outside of the garment. Top-stitched hems need to be pressed along the stitching to set the stitches down into the fabric.

INDEX

ACKNOWLEDGEMENTS

To the courage of Jaspar and Alice.
Many thanks to Chrissie, Michael, Emma and Karen, to Louise and Claire, to Amy and Katie at Pavilion, to Lisa Tai for her great work and to all our wonderful customers who recognize and embrace our mission.

MERCHANT & MILLS

Merchant & Mills is a company on a mission to return high end fashion to its rightful owners; you, the sewing public. We have a great respect for craftsmanship and the importance of quality in construction, cloth and tools. We employ strong graphic design and bring meticulous attention to all our endeavours.

Seasoned dressmaker Carolyn Denham is the driving force to get you all sewing. She cuts the patterns, sources everything and keeps order. Partner Roderick Field makes sure the Merchant & Mills philosophy is properly expressed in words, pictures and brand identity.

Merchant & Mills is stocked by high end stores from New York to Tokyo including Liberty, London and the Victoria and Albert museum.
merchantandmills.com

All photography by Roderick Field.

First published in the United Kingdom in 2015 by Pavilion
An imprint of HarperCollins*Publishers*
1 London Bridge Street
London SE1 9GF
www.harpercollins.co.uk

HarperCollins*Publishers*
Macken House
39/40 Mayor Street Upper
Dublin 1
D01 C9W8
Ireland

Copyright © Pavilion Books Company Ltd 2014
Text and pictures copyright © Merchant & Mills

Distributed in the United States and Canada by Sterling Publishing Co., Inc.
1166 Avenue of the Americas,
New York, NY 10036

ISBN 978-1-90939-741-5

A CIP catalogue record for this book is available from the British Library.

20 19 18 17 16 15 14

Reproduction by Mission
Printed and bound in China by RR Donnelley APS